**W9-DFW-320**

*H. H. Bradshaw*

# 4 × 4 Leadership and the Purpose of the Firm

The Haworth Press, Inc.

# 4 × 4 Leadership and the Purpose of the Firm

# HAWORTH Marketing Resources
## Innovations in Practice & Professional Services
### William J. Winston, Senior Editor

New, Recent, and Forthcoming Titles:

# 4 × 4 Leadership and the Purpose of the Firm

H. H. (Pete) Bradshaw

The Haworth Press
New York • London

HD
57.7
.B72
1998

The Haworth Press, Inc., 10 Alice Street, Binghamton, NY 13904-1580

Cover design by Marylouise Doyle.

**Library of Congress Cataloging-in-Publication Data**

Bradshaw, Pete.
    4 × 4 leadership and the purpose of the firm / H. H. (Pete) Bradshaw.
       p.   cm.
    Includes bibliographical references and index.
    ISBN 0-7890-0443-7 (alk. paper).
    1. Leadership. 2. Decision-making. I. Title.
HD57.7.B72 1998
658.4'092—dc21
                                    97-37012
                                        CIP

# CONTENTS

# ABOUT THE AUTHOR

**Howard Holt "Pete" Bradshaw** founded Organization Consultants, Inc. (OCI) in 1972, a company that has been designated three times as one of the 100 leading consulting firms in North America. Before becoming president of OCI, he worked for AT&T as a research psychologist and manager. In 1967, he joined Celanese Corporation's fibers group headquarters in Charlotte, North Carolina, soon becoming manager of the company's internal consulting division. The author of numerous management and leadership publications in over a dozen different journals, Mr. Bradshaw is the author of three books and editor of *The Journal of Managerial Issues*. Bradshaw is certified by the Institute of Management Consultants, and his biography appears in Marquis' *Who's Who in America*. He is currently Adjunct Professor in the Babcock Graduate School of Management at Wake Forest University in Winston-Salem, North Carolina.

# Foreword

If you like people who are at once civil and articulate, but will also let you know what they think, then you will like and value this book. While I would hope that it is not "Pete" Bradshaw's last book, it might well be regarded as a compendium of the insights and wisdom gained by an academically well-educated and trained (Yale and Duke) CEO and leader who founded a quarter of a century ago what, though relatively small, has been rated among the nation's top 100 management consulting firms.

As a consultant, the author's advice to clients has always been distinguished by the fact that it is research-based and therefore theoretically sound. That, of course, should please his readers who are academics. However, what should please those who actually manage and lead organizations—I count myself in the camp of those who opine that it's often hard to pull managing and leading apart—is that "Pete" Bradshaw also honors decisions and actions that result from reflecting on what can be learned from paying attention to one's experience, seasoned generously with a healthy dose of common sense.

As you, the reader, start your way into this book, I would caution you against a possible premature impression that what you will be getting here is "old wine in new bottles," triggered early on perhaps by Pete's usage of the concept of *trade*. Stick with what he is saying and you will understand that the word *trade* was not idly chosen. It "fits." It "works," as does the whole book . . . most especially, for anyone who has "been there" in managing and leading the essential human activity called *trade*. Bradshaw clearly knows what he is doing here.

In my profession, one is inundated with flyers from publishers regarding new books on management topics. The language describing what reading them will do for the reader is generally extravagant. I have tried to avoid following suit in that regard, but I will hazard the prediction that this is a book that is likely to be passed around among folks who are committed to making things work better in and through the workplace.

*Robert W. Shively*
*Professor,*
*Babcock Graduate School of Management,*
*Wake Forest University*

# Preface

For over twenty-five years I have earned my living largely as an advisor and counselor to leaders of organizations who are primarily, but certainly not exclusively, the leaders of public and private business organizations of almost every size and purpose. The reason for every assignment has been a leader's personal commitment to initiate and achieve some significant organization change. The average duration of intense, personal focus with each client executive has been about two years. Quite frequently the process recycles when the particular leader confronts new challenges in his or her original or different role. Often, too, my associates and I carry out a variety of additional activities that we believe will enhance the likelihood that the leader-driven changes will succeed. Thus, we develop considerable awareness of the organization's vulnerabilities and competencies throughout the hierarchy. We factor those facts and perceptions into presentations, conversations, suggestions, and explorations with the organization's leaders.

This is a description of what senior organization leaders think about, what they do, and why they seem to do it, written from the perspective of a participant and observer. Some years ago I began to notice in working closely with senior leaders that certain patterns recurred time and again. So began the testing and refining of these emerging views with executive clients and finally the development of the patterns and models described here. The book is much more akin to a naturalist's observations and search for order than a developed theory of organizations in general or business organizations in particular.

Though most senior leaders I've worked with seemed to use something very close to the thought processes described in the book, very few of these often intuitive executives were able to clearly articulate what they fretted about, what they did, or why. When presented with the model, a common reaction has been, "Yes. That is just what I do and the sort of thinking that goes into it, but I never thought about it this way before."

The research literature was not very helpful in trying to define and describe what leaders concern themselves with at an organization level. There is a large body of research that describes the styles, concerns, and approaches of effective supervisors and even managers. From OSS (Office of Strategic Services) team leader selection in the 1940s, the Ohio State studies of the 1950s, and much more sophisticated measures and models today, we know a lot about the concerns, skills, and outcomes achieved by supervisors and managers. We know very much less about what top-level leaders think about and do. I have found little of what is known about management and supervision to be particularly relevant or meaningful when the focus is executive leadership. Indeed, I am now convinced that management and senior leadership represent two quite different ways of thinking and exerting influence on complex organization systems.

There certainly are very useful and enormously insightful books and articles by such authors as Kotter, Lawler, Levinson, and Ohmae; but, as far as I can find, there are few explicit models or encompassing theories about what top leaders actually do to initiate, energize, and direct change effectively. This book is an effort to propose and explain one such theory in the hope that it may help us all better understand this vital, elusive thing called leadership.

# Acknowledgments

It takes people of uncommon persistence, vision, and sometimes courage to sustain successful enterprises. I want to thank those talented executives who, for over twenty-five years, have allowed my associates and me to help them improve the effectiveness of their organizations. They have all contributed to the ideas examined in this book.

I am indebted to my friends and partners in the firm—especially John Keller and Glenn Williams, whose extraordinary wisdom, skills, and insights inspire my admiration and mark them as among the very best. Most particularly, my thanks go to Sue Funderburk, our superb practice manager for over two decades.

Anyone who seeks to understand the leadership processes of complex and dynamic organization systems owes an enormous debt to the work of many theorists and investigators, past and present. Of these, I want to single out for special thanks Professor Bob Shively of Wake Forest University for his helpful critique and suggestions at every step.

Finally, it could never have happened without the ceaseless love and encouragement of my wife, Loretta.

# Introduction

Few accomplished organization leaders or individual exemplars are equally effective managers. The very best managers rarely become superior leaders. These two statements are counter to the beliefs and assumptions that support many advancement decisions and much management education.

Certainly, managers can and do provide leadership within a limited domain, and leaders often closely manage some specific activity of particular interest or importance. Leadership and management are both required for sustained organization success. But they are not the same, however, nor are they simply different points on the same linear continuum. Management and leadership are fundamentally different in kind, not just in degree. The scales and success criteria are different. This book is about how executive-level leaders think, and what they focus on to create and guide organization change.

Successfully leading any organization demands intelligence, vision, and focus of a high order. Courage and a realistic self-confidence help, too. The number, complexity, and interaction of influencing factors is enormous, and unlike some other professions, there is no codified library of immediately applicable rules, findings, and precedents. Nor are there many systematic theories or systems of guiding concepts and methodologies. Anyone who studies the research literature about organization leadership will soon recognize that there is a considerable body of largely disconnected, discrete findings not evidently linked by any encompassing theory or system of related ideas. We know a lot more about supervision and management than about top-level leadership.

This condition should not be surprising, for the deliberate study of organization leadership is only a few decades old. So are most of our very limited models and theories. To be sure, there are valuable diaries, biographies, and case studies. There are many important analytic texts that cover technical or functional applications, such as product costing techniques or effective advertising parameters. And there are important books that describe how to implement major interventions, like total quality, self-managed groups, or process reengineering. Business schools teach elegant quantitative techniques and a close analysis of necessarily simplified case studies. All of these are useful contributions toward understanding the enormously complex process of organization leadership. But they do not tell us much about the implicit and explicit models top leaders employ to guide their thoughts, plans, and decisions.

The long-accepted model is a single scale, a linear path with workers at one end and executive leaders at the other. Supervisors and managers of many kinds and levels are assigned roles somewhere in between. I am convinced that this model is fundamentally flawed, that management and executive leadership represent two separate and largely independent ways of perceiving and thinking, which derive naturally from different models, conceptions, and styles of thought.

In my experience, executive leaders typically possess an extraordinarily persistent focus on some organization destination, however fluid the path and indistinct the end point. These leaders concentrate on moving their organizations toward some future, and often elusive, image of what the place can and should become. Possibly a result of personality or perhaps because executive leaders are often psychologically and financially secure, their destination images seem to focus on the organization's future condition rather than on their own.

The most effective managers I have known are just as intelligent and tend to focus just as tightly—not on an organization destination but on the pragmatic uses of formal and less formal processes. Their primary concerns are the incremental tactics intended to yield relatively shorter term, more defined outcomes.

The concerns of executive leaders and managers are complementary and necessary, but they are quite different in focus and intent. For managers, key interests are typically organization and interpersonal process and, often, personal positioning; executive leaders are primarily concerned to achieve some organization-wide destination or temporary end state. This destination may be expressed in financial terms but is more often described by valued behaviors such as how the place and its people ought to act and how the organization should be structured—its main components, purposes, and linkages.

At the core of most leader-imagined destinations is trade and the consequent value of the enterprise. How must we act and what must we become to increase the chances for whatever I/we decide is successful trade? That is the single question, the destination, that most dominates the concern of senior-level leaders. That destination is the magnet that most attracts and engages executive leader interest, influence, and power.

Every profession has a more or less clearly defined purpose, an expressed reason to exist that its practitioners expect will provide personal meaning, cohesion, and esteem. Success will be variously defined by individual practitioners in terms of personal wealth, helping others, honor, recognition, or some other accomplishment. But those admitted to the profession typically agree with the stated purpose. For physicians, it might be health and the relief of suffering. For attorneys, the agreed purpose might be justice or fairness. For engineers, an agreed mission might be to apply technology to solve human problems.

I suggest that the leadership profession exists to enhance trade between people and among the institutions they direct. It is an altogether honorable and extraordinarily demanding calling.

Who are these executive-level leaders? Leaving personal and psychological variables aside, at a practical level such leaders are defined by position and power. They are the people whose decisions can usually be reversed by no more than one other individual and a board of directors, if there is one. For example, if a vice president's decisions can be reversed only by the president or by the board, that individual is an executive leader. Sometimes it can be difficult to specify who the leaders are in complex or overcomplex organizations. In itself, this condition can pose serious problems.

Executive-level leaders have significant position and considerable influence. Most have in mind some conception of a desired organization destination, an identity at the core of which is likely to be increased trade. What fills the thoughts and musings of leaders is the daunting challenge summed up by a single question: How can I influence this organization to move toward what I want it to become?

Leaders know that only skilled, confident, and committed people can sustain the focused energy necessary to drive any successful organization change. So, they are intensely concerned about maintaining and enhancing key employee morale and self-esteem through such conditions as greater *achievement* opportunities, increased individual *power* and control, personal caring and *recognition*, and high *ethical* expectations. These are the four primary sources of self-confidence. But only in very small organizations can any leader personally and frequently explain the destination, clarify the focus, and directly impact the morale of more than a small proportion of employees. The personal reach of leaders is greatly restricted by time and space.

Successful leaders project a clear and consistent picture of a desired organization identity. They put in place conditions that increase the likelihood of desired behaviors through enhanced employee self-esteem. To accomplish these goals, a leader must usually turn to the enduring architectural components of any organization, components that the leader can directly and personally alter by the allocation or withholding of resources.

These architectural features exist in every business, although the form and shape of each varies enormously. For instance, every business has *assets,* whether patents, money, equipment, or reputation. Too, every company has *people* with particular motivations, skills, and styles, and there is some *organization*—the way things get done. Finally, every organization has reporting and other *systems* that may be simple or very elaborate. Every business, whether tiny or gargantuan, already has these four architectural features. Properly linked, specified, and engaged, they are the primary levers through which leaders can project their vision, hopes, and influence throughout the company. If so linked and carefully designed, these four elements will yield a strategic identity—a coherence that can powerfully and positively impact both employee confidence and customer satisfaction. The process of converting established architectural features into consistent and coherent levers of change is, perhaps, a leader's primary responsibility.

Changes in one or another of the four architectural components are also potent symbols and communication vehicles, for they are avidly watched and discussed by employees and customers alike. From such changes are often inferred executive intentions and future corporate direction. Wise leaders invest considerable thought and effort on every component-level change.

My experience is that most effective leaders try hard to develop a progressively clearer picture of their organization's proper identity, and they seek understanding and acceptance of their image of the path and selected destination. As a rule, that image is grounded on defining and then increasing successful trade. These leaders know well that to enable the firm to move with assurance toward that condition, committed, confident employees with reasonable levels of self-esteem are critically important. Leaders also know that they usually cannot personally and regularly influence more than a small handful of key people. They cannot, personally, project their vision and influence very far. Power has real limits. Four architectural components, available to every executive, provide the change levers to influence employee self-confidence and to move the organization toward the envisioned destination.

A necessary condition for approaching that destination is profitable trade that can only be attained by satisfying customers. Just as all of us, customers have *needs* and *wants, hopes* and *fears*. How closely products and services meet both needs and wants, allay fears, and promise to fulfill hopes determines their perceived value. Not only offered products and services but also every transaction and every point of customer contact has the potential for improving customer satisfaction. The result of satisfactory, personal contacts, together with goods and services that purchasers believe provide good value, will usually be high levels of *customer satisfaction* and opportunities for increased trade.

Ultimately, and for the longer term, only skilled people who gain self-respect from their work can assure high levels of customer satisfaction. The two are most effectively linked when often static organization components are deliberately converted into strategically coherent levers of change.

How leaders can more effectively direct and improve the trading performance and value of small and large organizations is the subject of this book. My goal is to present the outlines of an integrated, systematic model of business leadership as it is actually practiced at its best with the levers of change realistically available to executive leaders and the essential linkages to member self-esteem, customer satisfaction, and sustained organization performance. The following figure illustrates the various elements involved in trade and the interactions among them.

Despite enormous differences in style and background, most senior-level executives share a common purpose. The most effective seem to focus unremittingly on just a few elements and patterns of elements they correctly believe will lead to achievement. I invite the reader to personally test and expand the ideas, models, and linkages in this book through his or her own experiences. Detailed accounts in *The Wall Street Journal* and many business magazines also provide rich lodes of material for applying the models and concepts.

Three basic ideas, three concepts, are central to business and to this book. They appear many times and in a variety of contexts. The following definitions are my own.

> **Trade:** The voluntary exchange of funds, goods, and services of any kind among individual people and as they represent larger entities such as families, tribes, corporations, or nations.

> **Executive Leadership:** The art and process of acquiring, energizing, linking, and focusing resources of all kinds to increase trade, of using trade to enable continuous change and movement toward some desired destination.

> **Strategic Identity:** The soul of the enterprise, its purpose, meaning, and actual strategy in-use as understood and experienced by members and outside observers.

Fully effective executive leaders are not common, neither is understanding about how they do it. I hope that this book will contribute to our fundamental understanding of top-level leadership and will help those who will one day occupy those positions.

FIGURE 1. A Model for Successful Trade

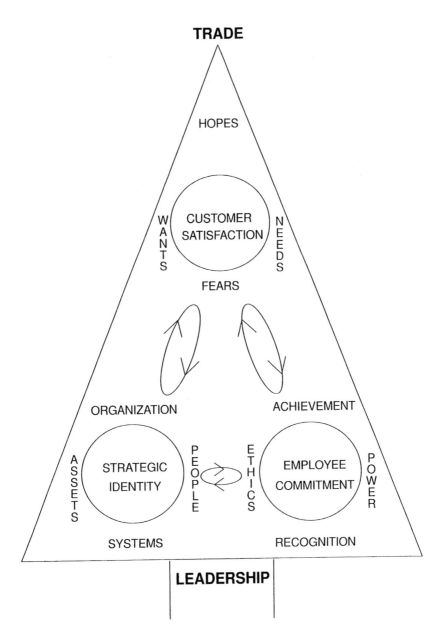

# SECTION I:
# THE DESTINATION—TRADE

FIGURE 2. The Business of Leadership Is Trade

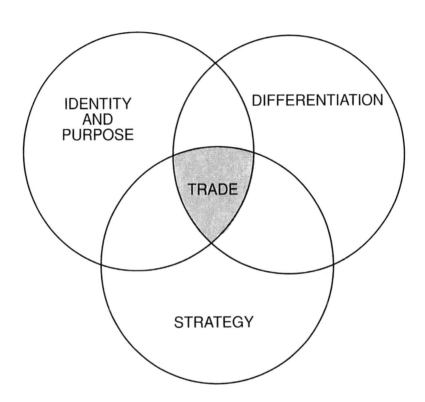

Our everyday conversation is filled with the ideas, activities, and language of business and, especially, of trade:

- Let's do a deal.
- Can we do some business?
- Let's horse trade.
- What's the trade-off?

These expressions have to do with trade, which means the actual or prospective exchange of something for something else. We have swap meets, cattle shows, and flea markets, where neither cattle nor fleas play much of a part, though once they did. Today, these kinds of gatherings are venues for unhampered buying, selling, and trading of nearly anything imaginable.

Business and most other organizations exist to trade and to do things that will lead to still more and better trade. Whether the entity is a professional practice, giant corporation, or an individual entrepreneur, it must trade to survive. That is its bedrock reason to exist. Nothing else, absolutely nothing, is as important. In this section, many kinds of trade are explored together with their costs and consequences. One important role of the leader is to cause assets to become resources for trade.

Later on, of course, costs and profits become vitally important. But first there must be trade. Certainly, not all business is good business, and not all trades are successful. But it is true that much of the time even an initially poor trade can later be made successful. A fair and honest trade has only a few defining characteristics, which have probably changed very little over the centuries. Even so, trade that is both successful and honest has associated costs that a leader must anticipate.

Ultimately, trade requires some sort of entity to provide the goods and services that will be offered. The leader of that providing entity, whether it is an individual, partnership, or company, must develop for it a clearly defined persona, in identity, and a sharp-edged image. The strategic identity can be a major asset. It should crisply tell potential customers, suppliers, and employees what you are, what you care about, and what you do. It makes little difference whether the particular institution is private or public, or profit/nonprofit making, large or small. Developing such a crisp identity demands of leaders an unrelenting focus and clarity about the organization's real stock-in-trade. In recent years, a good many firms and even whole professions have lost some definition. Just as looking through a poor quality lens yields a fuzzy, indistinct picture, so also have our understandings about some important firms, professions, and institutions become blurred. We aren't sure anymore exactly what they are, what they do, or why they exist. They have lost their once compelling and sharp-edged identity. Members of such organizations often describe a similar, out-of-focus work climate.

In contrast are entities, firms, and organizations, whose purpose, mission, and identity are crisp and coherent to most of us. The Red Cross and Salvation Army come to mind among the nonprofits, as do a number of exemplary business organizations such as Coca-Cola and Ford. A leader has no more important purpose than to maintain, enhance, or if necessary, dramatically recreate the organization's strategic identity. Leaders must avoid any dissipation of focus, assets, and effort. Long-term trading success absolutely depends on it.

One way to enhance an organization's trading muscle and to crisply define its strategic identity, is to separate and to differentiate that organization and its offerings from others. At a practical level, eight primary strategies seem to be the most commonly used. There are many successful blends, of course, especially in very large enterprises. Without a successful differentiating strategy, though, the thrust of any organization will start to blur in the eyes of its customers and, most important, its employees. Simply stated, neither will know what to expect—or what is expected. When that happens, trade will inevitably falter.

Sheer size is not the issue. A tiny systems programming shop, a law firm, and a huge, multinational corporation are alike in that all three require effective, confident people. They need people who know how to develop, produce, and deliver, and who want to. Whether the workforce is one or one thousand, there is no substitute for a clear and persistent focus on purpose, on strategy, and on differentiation. As shown in the preceding figure, all three are essential for long-term trading success.

Large organizations have great inertia that often carries them through failures that would sink a smaller or less wealthy enterprise.

Even so, every trading entity for success depends upon satisfying its customers. For almost every product or service, there are plenty of alternative providers who are anxious to serve your less-than-satisfied customers. There are also many potential customers who are vigorously seeking reliable sources for all kinds of goods and services.

Successful trade requires that these primary factors are connected and interconnected through a variety of potent linking techniques and methods. For instance, people will be more effective when they can clearly see their personal contribution to the identity, purpose, and strategy of the firm and to the satisfaction of its customers.

A crisp, strategic identity is essential to successful trade. It can be achieved through a variety of differentiation methodologies and a variety of linking techniques. Behind it all is the elusive and absolutely vital ingredient of executive leadership charged with the responsibility of moving the enterprise toward increased trade.

# Chapter 1

# The Purpose of Business

*The fundamental bond that unites men into society is the interpersonal exchange of goods and services.*

—Ludwig Von Mises

Humans are wanting animals. Whatever we possess, you and I, we want more. Or we want something simply different. My car is perfectly adequate, but I want a new one. My home is more than sufficient, still I want better. Present me with a pay raise, and in a few weeks I ask what you have done for me lately. Whatever the ancient era, culture, or site studied, archaeologists find undeniable evidence of trade. Watch a group of young children play: before long, someone will initiate a trade or swap, though it may look more like a takeover.

The expression of human wanting is trade. That is how most of us get more or different or better than whatever we have. The elements of trade have changed little over the centuries; what defines a fair and honest trade today probably always has. As I define it, *Trade* is "the voluntary exchange of funds, goods, and services of any kind among individual people and as they represent larger entities such as families, tribes, corporations, or nations." An honest trade has just a few defining characteristics. If any are violated, the trade is less than fair.

1. Whatever is to be exchanged must be demonstrably and substantially owned or controlled by each exchanging party.
   - If you're going to trade, "it" must be yours to dispose of.
2. Neither party to a trade may be coerced or forced by any other entity, whether individual, corporate, or government. Both parties must have the capacity to understand the trade.

*15*

- No third party coercion is ever fair for it distorts individual judgment and freedom.
3. Whatever is traded must be delivered where, when, and in the condition agreed upon.

All business is trade. Not trade in some general sense, but a specific exchange of something for something else. At bottom, every business transaction is nothing more, or less, than a swap. Every business and many nonprofit organizations exist solely to make advantageous trades. Despite high-sounding mission statements and pronouncements, no business exists to create jobs, be a good corporate citizen, or to create new products. It doesn't even exist to serve its customers. Those are tactics and strategies. The place exists to trade successfully. That is how wealth is created.

Somehow, many managers, professionals, and yes, business schools have developed a gauzy, filmy picture of what business really is. As a result, we have some giant corporations floundering aimlessly and highly acclaimed schools teaching ever more elegant ways to calculate marginal details. Banks and other financial institutions regularly loan huge sums to organizations without ever understanding why and how the borrower really exists. They do not understand what the borrower really has to trade, for what, and to whom. The savings and loan debacle of the 1980s resulted, in large measure, from just such ignorance. The recent derivatives trading failures are further examples.

Every important transaction between two or more people, or entities like corporations, is a trade, a swap, an exchange. Each party has something the other wants whether money, physical things, or a less tangible value such as service, status, or caring. That is all business is—trade and the continuous positioning of the organization for more and better trades. In recognition of this, a very large, worldwide industry has developed made up of firms that barter excess inventories of all kinds. Two examples include advertising space for office equipment and machine tools for real estate.

A disinterested observer of a particular trade may wonder why one or both parties would agree to what appears on the surface to be an unequal or even absurd swap. The appearance of absurdity is sometimes unreliable because each party is, usually, making the trade in what is then evaluated to be his or her best interest. Later on, of course, either or both participants may come to regret the trade. But at the time, it seems sound to both parties.

The outside observer rarely knows how each of the trading parties truly assesses his or her best interest. An outsider, including a government agency, cannot usually have a fully informed judgment about the relative merits of the trade as evaluated by each of the two parties. Outsiders should usually stay out.

Personal relationships are also trades; each party expects something he or she wants from the relationship. Outsiders may not understand why a particular relationship exists, but it is certain that each of the parties is receiving, or expects to receive, something valued. If that "something" becomes less valued or less available, the relationship will become less satisfying. Unless "something" else of equal or greater value emerges in the relationship.

Every human interaction, beyond the most transient and superficial, is a trade of some kind. The same is true for transactions by human inventions such as corporations, nations, and partnerships. Ultimately the purpose of any for-profit business or professional group, such as a law firm, is to establish conditions for one or a series of successful trades with outside individuals or entities. Every important business function exists, or should exist, to facilitate successful trades.

For instance, the research and development group exists solely to create new products or services to trade. Even pure research organizations exist in the hope of successful trades in the future. Manufacturing exists to produce things to trade. Accounting exists to keep the trading scorecard and to collect the results of trades through the accounts receivable department. Any business function that does not demonstrably and measurably facilitate trades and swaps, or that does not clear away obstacles to trade, should be closely examined. Trade is the sole purpose of business, whether the business is a giant corporation, an individual provider or a professional service group. Trade is the only way to create wealth.

All of this may seem obvious, but my observation of actions in plants, offices, clinics, and board rooms suggests that the obvious often needs considerable attention.

The defining purpose of any business is to exchange something—products and services—with some other person or entity. In return, the business gets something it wants that the other party is willing and able to give up.

The same is true for professions such as medicine, consulting, law, and religion. Only the nature of what is exchanged is somewhat different, not the basic process. At bottom, such practitioners offer to use their skills to help reduce or avoid pain, fear, and anxiety. Pain and fear reduction are very powerful incentives, which explains, in part, the high esteem often accorded these professions. In return for their best efforts, practitioners are given wealth and recognition. What they offer is usually less tangible and less pre-dictable, but no less real, than the products of General Motors or McDonalds. Doctors, lawyers, and the clergy, for instance, offer caring, hope, and their best efforts. They don't offer warranties or guarantees, and there is no reliable consumers' guide to rely upon in selecting a particular practitioner.

What is offered for trade by the professions is usually qualitatively different from the products of a factory. In some cases, though, the difference is becoming blurred. For instance, some leading car dealers offer much more than cars for sale. They promise and deliver to their customers extraordinary service, caring, and help at any hour. Try getting that from your physician. Some lawyers now offer generic, estate-planning packages that look very much like an assembly-line product from a factory.

The fundamental, underlying purpose is trade, whether the offering is a car, less pain, or the hope of salvation.

$$A \times PP = T \rightrightarrows W$$

Assets times performing people equals trade. Neither alone will result in successful transactions. Both assets and people, who can and will perform effectively, are required. Trade, in turn, *may* result in the creation of wealth but not necessarily. Many trades are not profitable or successful.

Assets take many forms. If primarily money, the organization might be a bank, insurance company, or other financial institution. For many organizations, the assets are largely intellectual such as specialized knowledge, skills, and patents. Land, property, brand names, physical equipment, and systems are assets and so, sometimes, are intangibles such as the organization's history and reputation in the market.

None of these kinds of assets will result in trade until someone does something with them. Only performing people, among them the leaders, can do that. Only people can buy, sell, rent, deliver, or create.

Leaders are largely responsible for converting assets into productive resources and, ultimately, into a coherent, cohesive strategy. They must determine the organization's structure and acquire the necessary reporting, analysis, and control systems. Perhaps most important, leaders are responsible for staffing, for hiring and retaining the kinds of motivated, skilled people they believe will best transform assets into successful trade.

Except in small organizations, top leaders can have only marginal influence on the performance of the day-to-day tasks that will result in trade. As a practical matter, a top-level executive can personally and directly influence the actions and attitudes of only a handful of subordinates. That is the reason why a healthy level of employee self-confidence is so vital at all levels and in all functions. Without a confident sense of self-respect, performance will falter and so will trade—despite the exhortations of leaders and deployment of large capital assets. Leaders have no more important responsibility than actively managing employee self-esteem through the organization elements and processes they can personally and directly impact. In my experience, the skills and determination of self-motivated, competent people are usually the most important components of successful trade. Healthy self-respect is vital to trade. Interestingly, successful trade, in turn, enhances participant self-esteem.

Imagine two people who have just traded goods with each other. Each experiences a sense of *accomplishment*, a major aspect of self-esteem. Each gave up something valued for something desired even more. The process of coming together, examining the goods, and negotiating a swap (the deal) is clear *recognition* that each is at least temporarily important to the other. Providing that there is no outside interference, each trader is powerful and can influence the terms and even *control* whether the deal takes place. Depending on the items, processes, and purposes of the trade, important values and *beliefs* may be validated. These are the primary components of self-respect. Trade depends on self-esteem and also enhances it.

I was once a member of the board of directors of a small company in trusteeship. The board served and represented the estate of the founders and, indirectly, the eventual beneficiaries of the estate. The company manufactured and sold a line of closely related proprietary products to the electronics industry and had been continuously profitable for many years. Quite suddenly, a much larger competitor appeared with products that looked and acted exactly like ours. Laboratory analysis showed identical composition, and our competitor's very low pricing looked like an effort to take over the market.

A disinterested outsider might have urged us and the company to sue for patent infringement, to dramatically reduce prices, to quickly develop new products, or all three. These were certainly among the choices, along with several others, that top management and the board considered at length.

The disinterested observer, though, could not have known that the patents we held were doubtful in some jurisdictions and would be expensive to defend. Nor could the observer have known that the beneficiaries, the eventual owners, had no interest in the business and wanted only the maximum possible cash from the company. They wanted money, and they wanted out.

Without this knowledge of the facts and the emotions involved, the trades made by the board and top management might have seemed downright silly. From the perspectives of both the owners and employees, the choices made by the board were ultimately successful. Every alternative considered represented a trade, some better than others. We tried to make the best swap we could through a merger with another of the company's primary competitors. In this case, the acquiring company had a complementary product line, about the same customer universe, and the deep financial resources needed to protect the patents and to develop new products.

At one level a "good" trade, purchase, or exchange is one that gets you what you want in return for something you are willing and able to give up.

## SELF-RESPECT AND CONFIDENCE

At another level of analysis, a "good" trade brings with it a feeling of achievement and accomplishment, one of the components of individual confidence. At the same time, a "good" trade, a good deal, allows us to feel that we are in control, that we are powerful and able to influence others to do what we wish, another source of self-esteem. In some trade situations, such as acquiring a company, negotiating a labor agreement, or making a large sale, the "trade" can also mean considerable individual recognition and a sense of increased personal importance. One's primary beliefs and values can also be significantly reinforced by some "trades." For instance, continuing one's education to become more skilled costs time, money, and effort. Becoming more proficient and effective might well be a strongly held value or belief. Honesty and meeting one's commitments are other examples of beliefs or values that can be demonstrated and reinforced during a trade.

At this level, a "good" trade can provide satisfaction of one or more of four strong human desires that add up to self-respect and confidence:

1. Achievement and accomplishment
2. Control and influence
3. Recognition and importance
4. Expression of basic values and beliefs.

When most of us experience such feelings, we accept and like ourselves. We approve of what and who we are. For most, there is no more powerful need than to approve of, like, and respect the person we are. A "good" trade enhances the self-esteem of participants because it increases positive self-evaluation from one or more of the four sources briefly listed above. A truly "good" trade increases the self-respect of all key trading parties and their overall satisfaction with the outcome. It greatly improves the chances of future trades among the same people.

The more that an exchange of goods or services engages all four esteem sources, the more positively the trade will be evaluated by participants. The more nearly equal the resulting self-esteem income between (or among) the parties, the more likely are future transactions. For despite legalisms and public postures, institutions do not trade. People do.

Trading is certainly among the oldest and most fundamental of human transactions. Trade has always served far more than a linear or simple economic function. It is a primary vehicle for meeting the powerful human wish for self-respect and self-esteem. Man is, indeed, a wanting animal and trade is the primary vehicle for meeting many of his needs and wants. The single unchanging purpose of every senior business executive is ultimately to facilitate and enhance trade.

# Chapter 2

# Investment, Speculation, and Other Trades

All business is fundamentally a constellation of trades. Some are sequential, one leading to another incrementally depending on results. Research based companies such as pharmaceuticals or oil exploration are typical. Each decision to invest time and money depends to some extent on the successes, or lack of them, of previous decisions. Every such investment is a trade. Someone decides to swap or trade the time of skilled researchers, laboratory costs, space and equipment use, the use or development of systems, and other valuable considerations. Those who make the trade are perhaps the vice president of research, the CEO, or even the board of directors. They make the trade of scarce, expensive resources in the hope of a significant discovery that will lead to a useful, safe product and, finally, to sales. These people make a judgment, together or individually, that the trade of company or department resources will at some future time result in a gain that benefits them. Viewed this way, any investment may be defined as a trade where the complete transaction will be completed, for good or ill, sometime in the future. A trade where one party immediately commits resources without knowledge of what the other side of the trade will be is more risky. We call this kind of trade an investment—sometimes speculation and sometimes research.

A familiar example is a state lottery. You commit resources (money), in the belief that the system used is honest and in the hope of enormous benefit in the future. You have no control over the process or the outcome and can have no further impact once the investment is made because your money is gone. This is among the most speculative kinds of trade.

Consider the earlier pharmaceutical example. Certainly, the trade in that situation is risky. Little or nothing of value may result from the investment, and the resources previously committed may be largely lost. But unlike the lottery, the resources committed can be stopped at any point in the process by the traders—the executives involved. The loss can be controlled or at least contained to a known amount. Or, alternatively, the traders might seek to improve the likelihood of a beneficial trade by increasing the weight on one side of the scale. For example, they might employ more scientists, or transfer scientists from other projects to this one, or seek to buy or license technology and knowledge from others. Unlike the lottery ticket buyer, who is a pure speculator, the business trader is usually sure to retain some control over potential loss and at least one side of the trade. That is the difference between investment and speculation. The speculator gives up influence over both sides of the trade. The investor tries to retain influence over at least one side.

Assuming they decide to proceed with the research project, the pharmaceutical company executives have done far more than simply commit people, money, and equipment to the trade. These executives, and perhaps the board of directors, have made other trades as well.

For example, unless the company is awash in retained earnings, other projects and other possibly beneficial research investigations may be cut back or even eliminated to support the subject trade. The decision to cut back one or more other projects, each decision itself a trade, has important consequences. Continuity of effort is reduced—people are dislocated and become uneasy, to name just two.

One of the roles of an advisor to senior management should be to help clarify precisely the nature of trades being made. Often, it is desirable to slow down the rush to decide and the momentum to move vigorously ahead that sometimes develops. The purpose of caution and clarity is to help everyone better understand more precisely what the terms of the trade(s) really are. What are we giving? What do we get now? What do we hope to get in the future? And—is it worth the risk? In a word, is it a good trade?

Every trade is made in the hope and expectation of immediate or eventual gain. To at least some degree, almost every trade is also a loss even before any gain is realized and regardless of how large the final gain is. When a trade is made, something is given up. That something is possible opportunity; opportunity to conserve your resources and to make a better or different trade for what you have to offer. That is part of the risk/reward judgment. One clear risk is that the trade fails to yield the expected benefit. Another may be the risk of missed opportunity. For instance, once I have spent my available money for one car, I may not have the ability to buy another, and I have also lost the interest my cash would have earned. At a corporate level, every merger or acquisition limits opportunities for a different and possibly better trade. If there are staff size restrictions, hiring one person may prevent hiring a better candidate who appears later. Investing in one venture may preclude investing in others.

The consequences of a trade choice can be subtle and take many years to become apparent. An oil refining company invested heavily in state-of-the-art equipment that allowed far more profitable production of the firm's primary product, asphalt.

Everything worked as planned; margins were greatly improved. The enormous cost of the new coker together with its support facilities kept management tightly focused only on the kinds of trades that would pay for the massive investment. An important consequence was that several attractive alternatives were quickly rejected that, in retrospect, might have led to much greater and more lasting success.

Adding considerable trade muscle in one arena gobbled up psychological and financial resources that could have been deployed in others. Paying for the new equipment blinded management to better alternatives. As one executive put it: *"It was just great, but now I wish we'd never built the damn thing."*

Senior executives and directors have no more important responsibility than to engage regularly in detailed, dispassionate examinations of the organization's important internal and external trading activities and opportunities.

There is almost no limit to what may be offered or accepted for trade. Some interesting offerings appear in the daily newspaper. All manner of things and services are offered or sought. Money is offered for rent, i.e., for a certain rate of interest. Trades for vacation time in one house are offered for time in another. If newspapers had existed in other, ancient cultures we might have seen gigantic stones advertised for trade in the Pacific Northwest, buffalo hides in the Midwest and flint tools in many areas throughout the world. The services of shamans and other healers would certainly have been available for trade along with the military skills of warlike tribes. In fact, all of these kinds of trade did take place. Truly, the trade defines what we call business. Barter, without coercion of or by either party, is the purest example of business. Learn what an individual, group, or society trades for, and you know much about their primary motivations and beliefs.

Today, entire corporations of immense size and wealth trade to acquire still other corporations. Companies may be acquired, merged or engaged in joint ventures. Acquisitions, mergers, and joint ventures are nothing more than different forms of a trade; all are some kind of a swap. In every case, two or more parties each put something on the table, and a deal is agreed upon. The terms of the deal, though often clouded by legal wording, really specify who provides or does what, who gets what, and when it all happens. That is all that most contracts spell out—the conditions of the trade.

Less tangible assets and less obvious but valuable (to someone) considerations are offered for trade every day. Prostitutes offer sex and sometimes the temporary illusion of love, security, and caring. Other people offer to clean out our garages and rake leaves. The skill required is low; what is really being traded is their time and energy for our own.

A trade can promise and provide intangible but not less valuable considerations. Cruise lines offer to trade more than just a boat trip. They offer status and prestige, attentive care, freedom from everyday inhibitions, and the prospect of romance and adventure. Churches offer the promise of eternal salvation along with companionship, personal caring, child care, and a host of other possible benefits. Each of these entities wants money, time, or other assets in trade for what they offer. In some cases, one's personal attendance or specific behavior is a condition of the trade. Civic clubs and political parties offer their members fellowship, achievement, and the possibility of exercising influence and power. In return, most seek the expression of shared values, money, and active involvement in the work of the organization. Typically, any two of the three conditions will suffice for a successful trade.

So, what can be traded? At the very least, these:

- Things, of enormous diversity
- Money, or anything else that serves as an agreed upon medium of exchange
- Time
- Power, control, and influence
- Evidence of caring, concern, and affection
- Salvation, security, and the expression of many other important values and beliefs
- Prestige, status, and recognition from others
- Personal achievement and accomplishment
- Skills and knowledge
- The prospect of less pain and fear

All of these and more, whether objectively measurable or, just as concretely, experienced and felt, are possible trade goods. All are entirely legitimate.

The basic purpose and fundamental mission of every senior executive leader is to make and facilitate trades that include the services and products of his or her own organization.

## THE LEVEL FIELD

For any trade to be fully legitimate, a few conditions are required:

1. Each party must, in fact, own or control the disposition of what is to be traded including time, skill, tangible assets, and behavior.
2. Each party must have reasonable competence to understand what is being traded at the time of trade.
3. No outsider or third party trading may coerce either or both trading parties by force or threat. The judgment of the trading parties should not be forced by any others, including governments.
4. Whatever is agreed upon must be delivered.

There are, of course, many transactions that do not meet these standards. In my view such trades are not wholly legitimate. Because of possible uncertainty about one or more of these four conditions, we have invented the term "due diligence," and such awkward statements as "We will do our due diligence."

All that the term "due diligence" really means is to inspect and verify the conditions and merchandise being offered for trade. "Count and grade the beaver skins," as a Canadian friend says. Or, as my doctor advises, "See if the diploma reads Penn State—or the state pen." He's right. About 40 to 45 percent of the résumés circulating today are significantly false. Due diligence means be as sure as you can about what you are trading for and what you will receive.

Above all, making a successful or a "good" trade demands ruthless self-examination, a gimlet-eyed appraisal of what you will offer and of what will be received. The self-examination is necessary to understand what you really want and the likely real impact if you are entirely successful in making the trade. Will you, or the organization, really benefit? Or is ego, fear, status, or some other emotion really driving the trade? Will the trade seem beneficial six months or six years afterwards, when the excitement and other temporary feelings of the moment have dissipated?

My frequent observation, confirmed by others, is that many large trades ultimately prove to be dissatisfying to the principal figures. Actions such as buying or selling a company, taking a private company public, or launching a takeover effort are enormously exciting. Lots of energy, interest, and adrenaline are evident. There is a heavy sense of expectancy and anticipation. You can almost see the squadrons mass, feinting here and thrusting there. It is all very heady stuff, and little of it has anything to do with how useful and successful the trade will prove to be. Emotions take over and even strongly cautionary facts are ignored or denied.

*Another such victory and we are undone.*

—Pyrrhus

A longtime client executive who took his private company public told me of his experiences in a candid and painful interview.

The run up to the IPO (initial public offering) was the most exciting period of my life. God, it was wonderful! Then it actually happened, and I felt like a captain of industry. Our executives were counting their new wealth and acting like kids. It was just wonderful! The press painted me large, analysts called for interviews, and so did several national television programs.

All that declined over the next six months, or even less. Somewhere after the IPO, I began to wonder if it had been a good thing to do. Today (three years later), I know it was a totally lousy deal for this company and its people. Sure, some few of us became very wealthy, but it isn't fun anymore. Everyone knows our business inside and out. We can't maneuver like we could. Outsiders decide what we should do and can do. And outsiders decide how we're performing. Those of us who became very wealthy already had more than enough money before. Now, we're the kind of typically sluggish, bureaucratic company I used to abhor. I let us all get caught up in emotion. I set the train rolling and became the engineer. I derailed this company from what it could have been.

You tried to warn me, what, six or eight times? You came up here on your own nickel and pleaded with me to delay for a few months just to reconsider. None of us could hear.

This is a clear example of how the process of even a major trade like this can gradually become driven by increasing emotion and by such a strong commitment to "making the deal" that objective analysis and thinking completely fails to have influence.

Consider the trade and trade-offs in this example. There is a demonstrably strong company—a recognized powerhouse in its industry. It is privately owned, very agile, and responsive to its market. The managers and executives have achieved measured, high pride and morale all through the workforce. Regular employee opinion surveys conducted when the company was private, contain hundreds of write-in comments such as the following:

We're the best dog on the block. We're faster and smarter than the other guys.

There's not a lot of crap here. When we need to move, WE MOVE. We know exactly what our customers want, and we make it for them.

> The top brass come here (one of nine plants) a lot. I met (the CEO) and told him some of our problems.

Conversations with this company's employees and managers several years later show that the CEO's evaluation is widely shared. The IPO made a few people wealthy but degraded important aspects of the company's character.

> You don't see the top brass any more. There's a whole new army of corporate people who have no idea what this company is—or was. No, I don't come in on weekends like I used to.

> There's a lot of distance and bureaucracy now. Decisions take forever to get from corporate and there's not nearly as much freedom to decide and act in the field as there was.

The mood now is: *"Put in your time and do what you are told."*
This is hardly an unusual outcome when other purposes supplant the incentive, and imperative, to trade, when the once clear company destination has become fuzzy and indistinct. It is a typical result of major, top-down changes in key elements made with little concern for employee self-respect or for the once coherent strategy, understood by everyone, that gave meaning and purpose to the enterprise.

A large proportion of corporate acquisitions and mergers yield disappointing results. In many such situations everything changes rapidly: people, systems, the core organization, and sense of cohesive thrust. Typically, employee self-esteem is given only cursory attention. Some surveys of CEOs estimate that between 60 and 80 percent of acquisitions are, ultimately, failures. From many years of personal observation, I have to agree.

Piedmont Airlines was a highly respected air carrier for decades. Its employees were as proud and dedicated, and its customers as loyal, as any I have ever seen. At one point when jet fuel was very expensive, most airline executives were vigorously telling their pilots to use less engine power. Rebuilding aircraft engines is also very costly and must be done periodically depending on engine use. So, corporate officials issued low power orders to reduce expenses.

Piedmont's pilots were visibly proud to report that their vice president of operations resisted the industry trend. As one pilot told me:

Captain Smith said to be sensible, but to use all the power we need. What he said was, "We can buy engines all day long. If you need it, use it. You're flying the airplane.


When another carrier went bankrupt and its planes were lined up at a major airport awaiting a judge's actions, Piedmont saw an opportunity. Acting very rapidly, the company bought some of the aircraft at bargain-basement prices. The deal was done very quickly. It was negotiated by uniformed Piedmont Captains who had full authority to commit the company.

Profitable Piedmont Airlines was acquired by U.S. Air in 1989 in a move strongly disliked by most Piedmont employees and viewed skeptically by many customers. As employees saw it, senior executives became enriched themselves and became increasingly remote, shielded by an ever larger corporate staff. These executives demanded substantial employee pay cuts yet offered none of their own.

Years later, U.S. Air is only now showing a regular or significant profit. It has sold aircraft and may still face eventual disintegration; all because top executives forgot that the purpose of their organization is to trade, not to do deals that make a very few people wealthy. Organization morale and individual self-esteem is so low throughout the company that recovery, even if possible, will require many years. So will regaining lost customer loyalty and shareholder value.

Business process reengineering, or BPE as it is usually abbreviated, has reached the status of a business fad in the past few years. There is, though, nothing new about the basic processes that define BPE. Well-managed companies of all kinds have regularly altered their trade strategies, their systems, staff characteristics, and organization structures. Most often in successful companies the changes are incremental, not wholesale. They are always informed, and sometimes guided, by enormous amounts of feedback, formal and informal, from customers and from all corners of the organization. There is evident concern for employee feelings and a determination to both do the right things, and to do things right.

Hunt Oil Company confronted enormous change in the mid-1980s when it discovered oil in what was then North Yemen. Ray Hunt and his executives faced many questions:

- How do we grow a major international oil company inside of a largely domestic organization?
- How should the new venture be structured?
- What should the role of corporate be, and how should corporate be staffed?
- How do we maintain focus and provide resources to expand our other primary businesses, such as real estate, while driving the new oil venture?
- What kind of staff, what new skills, will we need? Where? When?
- Do all of our existing businesses fit the kind of worldwide trade strategy we must now develop?
- How can we maintain the historic values and strengths of our way of doing things while becoming different?

Clearly, Hunt people would need to pull all four change levers: company asset deployment, the structure of the organization, many reporting systems, and the acquisition of new staff and skills. They did so, but only after carefully requesting and including the views and suggestions of many employees at all levels and in virtually all functions. They sought and listened to advice and suggestions from trusted outsiders. Moreover, the change process extended over several years, and included regular, very candid management retreats. Everything was on the table for consideration. There were extraordinarily open and frequent communications throughout the company and extensive supervisory training. Hunt Oil became a much different organization, but in ways that deliberately enhanced and engaged needs for individual self-respect in the service of greater trade opportunities.

What Hunt achieved was a redesigned company, a new strategic coherence, but without the usual, and sometimes disastrous, organization chaos and destructive loss of self-respect that seems to accompany so many BPE and downsizing efforts.

Some executives may argue that to save a declining company it is necessary to pull all four levers at once and quickly. Perhaps so. The test is whether the reengineered organization is more able to trade successfully or whether its essential strength has been so drained that it is weaker than before the sudden upheaval.

# Chapter 3

# Purpose and Focus:
# Why Are We Doing This Anyway?

*It is the Gods' custom to bring low all things of surpassing greatness.*

—Herodotus

Probably the most frequent question I am asked by want-to-be entrepreneurs is some version of "What can I do, and how do I get the bright idea?" They often have no clear idea of what they will trade, the essential of every business. Nor have many inventoried their assets to develop the clarity of purpose required. And, of course, courage expressed is not the same as courage demonstrated. It takes guts to be an entrepreneur.

These earnest and often very bright people say they have the desire to start and run their own business. They profess to have the drive, energy, and commitment. All vigorously assert a willingness to work very hard and long, without much income, to get the enterprise started successfully.

But relatively few can express exactly what they want to do or how they will do it. There is little focus to their wish. Many seem to be running away from what they believe to be the ills of large corporations and the authority of others. To a significant degree, the expressed drive seems to be more a wish to avoid control by others than a true desire to "do it my way."

Just last week a thirty-five-year-old PhD (aeronautical engineering) visited to talk about how to start his own firm. After eight very highly paid years with a major aerospace firm, he badly wanted out.

The instability in defense and the inside politics are driving me crazy. It takes forever to get a simple decision. All we do is meet and talk. Everything depends on who you know and whether you are one of those anointed. The top execs have no idea what we do.

*What do you want to do?*

I want a place where I can do the advanced design work I'm trained to do without a lot of interference from people who don't know very much.

*What will you make or what will you sell?*

I don't see why we always have stop-start funding with a lot of begging and wasted time in between. I want to design better, more efficient shapes.

*Wings or what? (I know nothing about aeronautics.)*

Yes. Wings, surfaces and shapes of all kinds. Without a lot of interference.

*But if you start a company, your own funding will probably be anything but smooth. You'll also have to do a lot of selling, schmoozing, and cajoling with customers, suppliers, and especially your own employees.*

Isn't there some kind of business I can set up where I don't have to do much of that? Where I can do design work?

*Yes, you probably can. Are you willing, and is your family willing, to have a lot less income and fewer benefits as a subcontractor working at home? Can you tolerate some months without a paycheck? Are you prepared to take on some simple, low-level no-brainers just to pay the mortgage?*

I don't know.

You see the problem. Knowing clearly what you want to achieve and what you are willing to risk is not always easy or automatic.

In my experience, would-be entrepreneurs who are ultimately successful have a clear picture of what they want to trade and with whom. They have some idea of their possible market and competition. But mostly they think they know what their trade inventory should be, and they have courage. Never mind that many eventually successful entrepreneurs fail and start again. Every time they restart, devoted entrepreneurs at least think they know what they have to trade. Many eventually succeed. These people are not running away from anything. They positively seethe with desire to pursue their own dream, their destination. They know that for a time, at least, they will have little income and security. It is a trade they willingly make for the chance to develop and build a vision. The reality of that vision, if largely achieved, will become the stock-in-trade of a new business.

The sole purpose of any business or service-providing entity is to trade. The primary accountability of leaders is to help make or facilitate trades. When that bedrock truth eludes either beginners or established organization leaders for any significant amount of time, serious problems will follow. In large organizations the consequences may take years to become visible. In new or smaller companies, the results can be nearly immediate.

Sometimes it is obvious when the leaders of even a large, successful company act as though they have forgotten that it exists solely to trade. It has been reported that IBM once had an internal staff of about seventy full-time architects plus support people to design the firm's many handsome facilities. Typically, what was no doubt intended as a variable cost became, effectively, a fixed cost and thereby added to nonproductive, overhead expense. Nonproductive in the sense that this group of architects could not and did not facilitate or make any trade in IBM's real business. Neither did IBM's investment in its magnificent art collection. The same company, IBM, rejected the opportunity to trade in personal computers when it probably had the best chance of any corporation on earth to do so. It gave away the chance to trade in its main business, computing, while buying thousands of acres of land and constructing elegant, unproductive, buildings. That money could have funded the development and marketing of desirable products for trade. The result was a collapse in IBM's stock price and the tragic dismissal of thousands of managers and highly trained professionals. The financial and psychological cost can hardly be overstated, nor is it over. The firm's leaders allowed its once powerful strategic coherence to dissipate at one level and to become rigid and dogmatic at another.

All this is not to highlight IBM's past problems alone. There are dozens of examples in many industries. The point is that when the leaders of even a large and wealthy organization begin to become inflexible and focus not on trade, but on sideline issues, it is time to sell the stock or to take your talent and commitment elsewhere. The business of business is trade; nothing less can ensure success and survival.

Leaders of the U.S. auto industry nearly forgot that its job, its purpose, is to make cars for trade to consumers, to you and me. Many of the luxury U.S. cars of the early to mid-1980s were terrible in both design and quality. A few more years would have seen the end of at least one major manufacturer. Fortunately for us all, the industry rediscovered its purpose. It began making cars people wanted to buy. Company executives rediscovered trade as the absolute. Those powerful organizations have, like all companies, no other reason to exist.

Business executive and innovative automobile dealer, Carl Sewell, understands this. In his book *Customers for Life*, Sewell describes a lengthy menu of activities and investments undertaken in his businesses to enhance trade over the long term. For many years, I was an advisor to Sewell and his staff. The tasteful, immaculate facilities, expensive reporting and control systems, and clear statements about how every employee is expected to act, are some examples of Sewell's approach. Every such action, policy, or investment is, finally, intended and designed to increase trade. Because his businesses deal directly with the public, Sewell really sells much more than cars. A major investment in facilities is, for him, an appropriate strategy to increase trade. The same cannot be said for the many corporations whose thousands of opulent offices and buildings will never be seen by an ultimate consumer. These facilities have no positive impact on trade. Indeed, designing, building, and maintaining such facilities divert executive attention and absorb assets that could better be used to develop new and innovative products, make better quality offerings, and market more effectively—In a word, assets that could better be used to increase trade.

Large organizations alone do not make this error; it is not simply a matter of size. It is primarily the consequences of a loss of focus on the firm's strategic identity and coherence by senior-level executives and the reluctance of timid, uninvolved boards of directors to exert influence. Prior to its court-ordered breakup in the early 1980s, say in the 1960s and 1970s, AT&T was one of the largest corporations in history. At one time, AT&T and its subsidiaries had well over a million employees. For the most part, the company's units and executives were remarkably focused on their business, on trade, as the market and legal climate existed then.

With the exception of a few New York buildings and one or two research facilities, most AT&T offices and facilities were functional but decidedly spartan. There was a notable absence of bubbling fountains and other expensive accessories. But most units were not parsimonious when new product development or product quality issues were concerned. After all, the company heavily funded the Bell Telephone Laboratories and the work of its Nobel Prize winners. Where assets could be used effectively in the service of trade, even if problematic or years in the future, they were usually allocated. Activities that did not were very modestly funded, if at all. No, the issue is not simply size or corporate wealth. The issue is one of making the numerous, highly focused trade-offs needed to advance the likelihood, and the success, of trade.

Any company, any partnership, can lose focus on its primary trading purpose. The smaller the organization, the more rapidly the loss of definition becomes evident.

We once worked with a refrigerated-truck-body manufacturer. Nationally, this is a large and profitable market, and there are many competitors. Our client had an enviable reputation, low labor costs, and respectable facilities. In an effort to rapidly grow the business, the company's leaders undertook to bid on some exciting but completely unrelated products. During a six-month period, more and more factory time and space were devoted to developing the new product. Gradually, the best marketing, technical and crafts people were moved from truck bodies to the new product, none of which had ever been sold. The firm began to lose its longtime cohesion and coherence.

Predictably, serious quality problems began to develop with the truck bodies. Deliveries fell behind and costs increased as energy and assets were focused on the new, potential product. The owners borrowed more funds to expand the plant in the hope of many future sales of the new product. A year later, the firm, practically bankrupt, was sold to a competitor.

Loss of leader focus is a major threat to any organization. Large, comparatively wealthy organizations possess the credit lines, inertia, and outside scrutiny that can prevent collapse. Smaller firms often lack these advantages.

What has been said about the loss of focus shown by excess attention to physical appearances is equally true of the size and growth of corporate and other support staffs.

In my view, that of other observers, and, privately, by staff members themselves, many corporate support staffs are still too large. Few large organizations would suffer any loss of business if support staffs were reduced by 10 to 20 percent. Support people and their jobs, in this definition, do not demonstrably contribute to present or future transactions. Some staff positions are necessary for other reasons, but not nearly so many as there are. Many staff or support positions exist to perform tasks and marginally useful studies, or to run errands for senior executives. They have only the most remote connection with the business of the organization, which is to exchange. Some employees perform tasks that are necessary or legally required but still not a part of the core business. Increasingly, large and small organizations are contracting, or outsourcing such functions. Many personnel, legal and financial functions, among others, are now commonly contracted to other specialty firms. Cities such as Charlotte, North Carolina, are beginning to contract out many activities and services previously performed by city employees. The city's elected officials intend to focus city employees' efforts on a reduced group of core functions, those they deem to be truly central to the business of the city, such as public safety.

Nucor Steel is the third or fourth largest steel company in the United States. It is quite likely the most efficient producer of any company in the world in its competitive arena.

Ken Iverson, Nucor's chairman and CEO, has never let the company lose focus or wander far from its core strengths. Nor has he allowed corporate staff to distract, for there are only twenty-two people at corporate. Nucor won't need to delayer either, because there are only four management levels, companywide. Ken and his people constantly adjust the four levers. They add skills and assets, including entire plants, when and where needed; their systems are always being changed, and there is a continuous thrust to spearhead the commercial use of new technologies and new trade relationships. Only the basic organization and central identity of the company seem to remain unchanged. Probably because it is hard to think of anything simpler or more straightforward.

Oh, yes. There is no corporate airplane or executive dining room. The company's rented headquarters is in a suburban office park near several cafeterias where everyone eats. I chided Iverson a few years ago when he moved the corporate offices, then as now only twenty-two people, to somewhat larger quarters. He fumed that he would not have moved except that ". . . the damn records keep taking more space." Besides, his people negotiated an excellent deal—just as they do every time Nucor builds another steel plant.

Nucor is what many organizations hope to be after radical re-engineering and downsizing. Hope to be, but often are not.

Ideally, corporate employment reduction, euphemistically called downsizing or rightsizing, is much more than a simple attempt at immediate cost reduction. If it is only that, executives, shareholders and boards of directors are likely to be soon disappointed. The results will probably be short term and much more modest than expected. When such employment reductions represent a genuine strategy, at all levels, to pare the organization back to an effective trading entity, the outcomes can be gratifying.

Under such a deliberately chosen strategy, the purpose is not just to cut the number of employees, often unfeelingly described as "headcount" reduction. The goal is more than so-called delayering or rightsizing or business process reengineering. These short-term expedients often prove to have been serious mistakes. There is, in fact, published evidence that many executives believe that upward of 70 percent of such efforts as these fail. Over 150 executives who have been involved in downsizing and reengineering were asked to evaluate the impact. Over 65 percent said the results were quite disappointing. That is because such efforts often focus on short-term gain by eliminating people or on doing the same activities as before, just faster or more efficiently. We should not expect either uniform or significantly positive outcomes from efforts that do not focus on enhancing the trading muscle of the organization, its real purpose.

In contrast, Mercury Marine markedly reoriented parts of its large organization specifically to improve trade. As one example, they achieved spectacular and recurring financial improvement in their stainless steel marine propeller business. Propellers of this kind are highly technical in design and require quite substantial metal casting and machining skills. They are also a highly profitable line of business. Mercury's propellers have long represented the performance standard.

The problem Mercury executives confronted was dealer and customer dissatisfaction caused by the company's inability to produce enough propellers of the proper size and type for the firm's various worldwide markets. As a consequence, profits and orders had seriously degraded.

The solutions, for there were several, were designed and implemented by cross-function teams of production workers, supervisors, and engineers. They had the full support of Bud Agner, the Senior Vice President of Manufacturing. Bud knew that reducing cycle time was the key. To achieve that, everything else, like quality, had to be in place. The teams did not simply redesign or reengineer existing processes. Nor did they decide to cut employment to achieve temporary profit objectives. Instead, they adopted several parallel strategies that targeted upon exactly what dealers and the ultimate customers wanted. They concentrated on each step, from steel ingot to box. A great many processes were dropped altogether in casting, machining, inspection, accounting, information systems, and materials. Others were dramatically simplified, and a few were added. The fifty-year Mercury Marine culture had long dictated numerous reports, approvals, checks, and reexaminations. All required time. All required multiple checks, reports, inspections, and balances. The teams concentrated on satisfying the customer by rethinking the entire propeller business. Cycle times plummeted, quality increased, and customers bought and paid for a lot more propellers. You can't do business from an empty wagon. So Mercury people filled the wagon with exactly the products customers wanted, when and where they wanted them, and at a price they were willing to pay. Mercury people redefined the propeller business and achieved a consistent strategic identity that everyone, customers and employees, could clearly see.

Mercury concentrated on trade, not theory. The teams succeeded because they asked some basic questions and eliminated every activity and function that did not provide at least some of the answers and measurable value. The propeller group is now a largely autonomous business unit. Under Agner's leadership, Mercury's people asked some basic questions:

- What, exactly, do our customers want? When? Where? To do precisely what? At what cost?
- Where and how, exactly, can we meet these desires?
- How can we fix any problems, permanently?
- When and how will we know that we did so?

These are the questions of trade. The more clearly they are asked, the more objectively analyzed, and the more vigorously pursued, the more successful the business will be. The primary role, mission, and purpose of every top-level executive is to increase defined trade for the company or unit he or she represents and to clearly and persistently specify the path.

## WHAT IS A GOOD TRADE?

It all depends on what you want, what you have or can get, and, finally, what you'll give. The issues and questions are the same whether you are an individual or the CEO of a multibillion-dollar corporation. Very little else matters to business success and survival.

When a purchase of any kind is being considered, much more than the swap or the transaction itself is important. First, there is always the question of trust. Can the other party be trusted to carry out its end of the trade? Will the service or product be as I hope? Will it meet my needs? The courts are clogged with civil cases that hinge on this issue. The more complex or valuable the trade, and the more parties involved, the more it seems there are charges of violating the agreement by one or more parties.

A defense client of ours had a very serious problem. A complex aircraft, latching mechanism they purchased elsewhere for installation on their equipment was failing in the field. Their supplier was, apparently, in such desperate financial condition that it had substituted less expensive and weaker latch components in the one area that our client's people could not inspect. A cursory check of the supplier's finances would have rung the alert bell. But the supplier was small and the cost of the latches relatively minimal, so the verification was overlooked. Hopes for a long-term relationship disintegrated amid a lot of worry and unmet needs. Fear of repetition, if nothing else, has considerably changed the supplier qualification system.

Another concern that influences many trades is the hoped for or expected amount and history of help and service provided by each party after the sale or exchange. This is more than a simple concern over warranties. It is, again, a matter of hope and trust. Will the other party willingly, even eagerly, make it right? Even more than just complying with contract requirements, will each party try hard to make sure that the other is satisfied? For a particular end-use consumer, let's say a car buyer, the expectation of service after the trade is often critical to the initial sale. The consumer hopes and expects the dealer or factory to make good any defects. In business, there is often a much more complex set of expectations on both sides. Moreover, the expectations can extend over a very long time. Thus, each party expects, or at least hopes for, something more than just whatever is detailed in the agreement or contract. That is why intangibles like reputation, confidence, and values are so important in trade. No contract can cover every possibility; if it did, few would understand, let alone agree about, the meaning of all the legalistic words. As Sewell writes, "Find out what the customer wants, and give it to him." As a close associate of Ray Hunt says, "Shake hands with Ray and it's done. Whatever it takes is what will happen."

## WHAT DO YOU WANT?

In many ways, this is the most difficult question for an individual entrepreneur, a company leader, or a member of the board of directors. The more alternatives and the more options you have, the more difficult the choice(s). A closely related question in analyzing any trade or constellation of trades is assessing how much risk is comfortable for the person or group involved. I have advised and observed boards and executive-level committees for many years. Some are quiet, deliberate, and inclined to make few decisions and take even fewer significant risks. Sometimes, though, this polite, deferential style leads to an unspoken agreement to deny legitimate fears and to suppress conflict, especially if there is real opposition or implied criticism. Such groups often avoid seriously considering the very trades and even a defined destination that would most benefit the organization. In some well-publicized situations, such as Eastern Airlines, unspoken decisions *not* to act, have brought companies near collapse and even into bankruptcy.

By way of contrast, other executive committees and even boards of directors act more like a slightly unruly pep rally. There is palpable excitement and energy with vigorous discussion and debate. A lot depends on the style desired or allowed by the most senior person present, by the culture, or by another strong leader determined to raise key issues even if the group prefers to avoid them. That was surely one key reason for the decision of General Motor's board to buy out member Ross Perot. The management and board probably wanted no part of the kinds of trades Perot was pressing.

A vigorous, active board and executive committees can be enormous assets. Alternative strategies can be surfaced and energetically advanced. Every destination image is really a constellation of contemplated trades. So, such an involved group is very helpful in defining and keeping a crisp focus on trade, the business of the company.

There is a possible downside when an active, aggressive committee or board develops a steamroller style. An almost messianic psychology sets in. The pressures for conformity become just as potent as those in the kind of polite, nonconfrontational, and uninvolved group described earlier. When that happens, there is a sort of piling on; members vie with each other to up the ante and to appear even more aggressive in support of the emerging or prevailing direction. The consequence can be a loss of strategic cohesion and some highly risky trades. A number of corporate acquisitions and expansions, which are also trades, come to mind. A year or two after such maneuvers, many executives have privately, and sometimes publically, stated that the trades were unwise and even foolhardy. They had allowed themselves to be swept along by the excitement and glittering prospects. As an advisor, I sometimes feel the need to try to accelerate, challenge, and energize. At other times, my role becomes cautionary and restraining. The purpose, either way, is an attempt to bring about a concentration of well-considered choices and favorable transactions.

From what has been said, we can see that a great many senior-level board and executive level decisions are driven by emotions at least as much as by fact and analysis. This should not be surprising. Most important decisions involve too many factors, known and unknown, for any individual or any group to fully understand. I would judge that well over half of significant business choices are driven largely by emotional considerations. That's the nature of most important transactions and why deciding what you want to gain is so difficult. Add to that, there are usually a wide variety of personal agendas operating within every board, senior staff, and executive committee. For instance, the company president may want to preserve his or her job, or gain renown as a leader, or simply stay on until a particular level of personal wealth is achieved.

An inside board member may want to curry favor with the company president or board chairman. Or the board member may seek to establish a position as replacement for the president. Outside board members may simply want to preserve their income and board member status. Or they may feel a strong commitment to one or another constituency such as owners, employees, or the senior executives.

## WHY DO YOU WANT IT?

The point of this question is that choices made at top executive levels or ratified in the boardroom are just as emotionally driven as they are in organization life, generally. The existence and power of emotions coupled with the great uncertainty of any substantial transaction means that it can be very difficult to get clarity and agreement about what is *really* wanted from a trade and how it will advance the journey. If you have ever built or redecorated a home, you know how quickly emotions become attached to various choices and decisions. A home is, after all, a major trade for most of us.

Just as difficult in many business situations is deciding *why* the outcome of the proposed exchange is desired. Asking executives to specify *why* they want to spend money or commit other assets elsewhere can be frustrating for both of you. Incredibly complex chains of interlocked justifications, hopes, and myths are often the response. The more senior the level of the advocate, the more others will defer and accept rationales they suspect, or sometimes know, to be false. Unless some new factor or person intervenes, such elaborate rationales can develop a strong momentum, to the extent of being formalized as strategic plans—without even one person stating a caution or divergent view. The economic failure of the Edsel car and more recently the Cadillac Cimeron, whatever their other virtues, are examples, and so is the more recent Orange County, California, bankruptcy.

Just a month ago, a multibillion-dollar corporation quietly dropped year-long plans and design efforts for a very costly, multifloor, downtown office building. No one much below the level of vice president thought the expenditure wise, necessary, or remotely justified. When I questioned senior executives, most echoed the wildly improbable theme that if the corporate staff were spread over many vertical levels, communication and teamwork would somehow increase!

The real reasons for wanting an elaborate tower can only be guessed. Status, recognition, and visibility come to mind. Fortunately, the board of directors reversed its earlier decision. MCI's expensive and unfortunate decision to move to Colorado Springs was eloquently justified and explained by company leaders again and again. As reported contrary facts and advice from many sources were simply denied.

Unspoken and unacknowledged agendas and assumptions are the currency used to support many trades. Nearly every week we read in the business press about the efforts of companies to fight off an undesired purchase or takeover effort, often at great expense. Frequently, board members and corporate executives act as though they assume that continuation of the enterprise as an independent entity is an existential "good." They erect all kinds of so-called poison-pill defenses, seek to amass cash by selling units of the business, or borrow heavily to make the proposed takeover less attractive. The atmosphere becomes emotional and even frantic as the people involved behave like the officials of a medieval walled town under siege. Rarely in my experience does anyone dare to raise the question "Might it [the trade, the sale] not actually be better for the owners and employees?"

To be sure, executives of a company in serious financial difficulty may welcome a purchase offer, but otherwise, many do not. Once again, emotions and individual agendas have enormous impact on how the proposed deal is understood and evaluated. The question of *why* we really like or don't like the proposed exchange often slides by unasked and unanswered.

## *TRADE STRATEGY*

At the most basic level, there are at least two solutions to doing business successfully. First, offer what someone wants that no one else offers. Second, offer substantially the same products or services as others provide but with clear advantages to the customer that your competition does not offer.

The market rewards differentiation. When all offers are about the same, no one is likely to be especially rewarded. Differentiation is one key to successful exchanges and should be clearly reflected in the organization's asset deployment, its systems, people, and organization configuration.

The purpose of a particular business strategy and the measure of its success can be described and measured in many ways, for instance:

| | |
|---|---|
| Sales volume | Productivity and efficiency |
| Market share | Positioning for future trades |
| Staff morale | Increased owner value |
| Measured customer satisfaction | Proportion of repeat business |
| Profits | Number of new offerings |

For instance, suppose that, like Nucor, we can produce steel at the lowest cost in the industry through a cohesive, fully accepted productivity and efficiency strategy. For that to occur, the entire organization must be configured for efficient production; the right people must be in the right positions, assets have to be deployed, and our reporting and control systems must be exemplary. Success in achieving lowest production cost can allow for pricing our goods in ways that will clearly differentiate us from our higher-priced competitors. That differentiation can, in turn, produce higher profits. Profits are assets that can be used to enter a new business, purchase new equipment, or any other purpose that moves the company a step or two along the path toward the destination envisioned by its leaders.

Or, like Sewell, we might determine to develop a coherent, driving strategy aimed at achieving extraordinary levels of customer satisfaction. That means employing and continually expanding the capabilities of talented people, investing assets in appropriate plant and equipment, and creating highly responsive reporting and control systems. The repeat trades and higher margins that result from a base of highly satisfied customers increase the value of the enterprise for its owner(s), allow much higher than average compensation for employees, and permit a variety of new initiatives—initiatives that can make the company more nearly congruent with the hopes and visions of its leaders.

Piedmont Airlines achieved truly remarkable customer and employee loyalty largely by an intent focus on morale and service. Piedmont's founder and first CEO was convinced, correctly, that sales volumes, profits, and company value would follow.

Achieving a long-term differentiation strategy is both grounded on and strengthened by a strategic identity where assets, systems, the organization itself, and its people form a nearly seamless consistency, when the aligned architectural elements seem to present a unified statement about what the place is and does. One way to tell whether such strategic coherence exists is to separately ask leaders, employees, and customers to describe the firm. When they largely agree, you can bet that a coherent identity is in place.

A key component of such coherence and a primary requirement for successful differentiation is usually the assured self-confidence and skills of the company's people—its employees at all levels. When people have the internal, personal strength that comes from self-respect they can, and often will, make even marginal approaches work. Skilled, self-confident people are essential to achieve successful differentiation. Just as important, their sense of personal worth and value feeds back and greatly enriches the core, strategic identity of the enterprise.

Differentiation really means deciding how you are going to serve customers differently from your competitors. Over the longer term, differentiation also means determining how you will deal with employees so that your customers will be continuously delighted with the services and products you provide.

The would-be trader needs to be reasonably certain that he or she knows what is wanted and also what others are already offering. Just as important, great objectivity is needed to be sure that what we think are the extra advantages we can offer are, in fact, advantages as eva-luated by our potential customer. Many times I have seen senior-level executives convince themselves that a proposed, nifty change or addi-tion to product or service would be greatly desired by possible custom-ers. Sometimes the exciting changes are funded, produced, and introduced with no impact at all. Crystal Pepsi Cola is a recent exam-ple. It was introduced at considerable expense and withdrawn from the market after just a few months. It is exciting and even fun to join colleagues in championing some change, but often there is little or no improvement in trade. What looked so promising becomes a dud because no one asked the customer what was wanted, and no one in authority raised a cautionary flag. There are few more important executive responsibilities than to learn, firsthand, what your customers think of your products and what they want from your organization. Do it and you'll also learn much about your competition.

How else do you learn about what others are offering for trade? Look, ask, listen, acquire, and test. It is sometimes amazing how few company executives and board members privately purchase and use their own company's products or those of the competition. This kind of personal intelligence gathering doesn't work as easily for builders of airliners or office buildings, of course. But for many goods and services it can add valuable, firsthand knowledge. If my company made dog food and my dogs wouldn't touch the stuff, I'd like to know. And I would start informing and asking anyone who would listen. Depending on the company's structure, product de-sign or quality assurance might be my first stops. Market research or the product manager wouldn't be far behind.

One primary source of knowledge is the organization's personnel at all levels. At least some may know exactly what the competition is offering and how your products or services measure up. But these people are rarely asked. Your customers probably know a lot about your competition's products and services. They certainly know about yours, and they know what features or factors are true advan-tages in their own experience. Your own suppliers and vendors are yet another source of the kind of information needed.

The information needed to increase the probability of successful trade exists and is available, if you ask and listen. Top leaders and even directors need to be personally involved in gathering such information and can deliberately empower others to share what they know in an accepting atmosphere. Wouldn't you rather have an employee or customer tell you honestly that one of your products or services is inferior, than to find out from the balance sheet? To a considerable degree, information is the engine of trade.

There are several primary trade-driving strategies, each with many possible variations. Probably no organization can successfully and vigorously pursue all, but some try. A rule of thumb seems to be that no executive team can stay focused for long on more than three or four strategies. At a practical level, few organizations can afford to adequately fund more than a handful of possible approaches. Too many thrusts in motion all at once can become distracting background noise and can weaken company cohesion. It is far better to follow one or just a very few approaches over a long period, than to adopt too many or for only short periods. The latter situation produces a serious lack of focus, unnecessary cost, and a feeling among employees and observers that an unfocused, ineffective management has, once again, embarked on a fad of the month.

The eight primary strategies described later in the chapter seem to be the most common in use. Each can be highly effective, especially if combined with no more than one or two others over an extended period. Very few organizations can focus long on more than a very few strategies, nor do they function well when the selected approach changes frequently.

Perhaps the most common failing I observe among top-level executives are indecision about and inattention to the company's selected trading strategy. It is in this arena that those in charge need to exert their every energy if the enterprise is to succeed.

## *SOME TRADE STRATEGIES*

A primary purpose of business strategy should be to define the firm's destination and, specifically, how the company or other organization will seek to exchange successfully. Some strategic questions that must be resolved include:

- Who, really, are our customers?

- What do they want?
- How can we meet those desires?

These questions should be asked and answered for every product, every service, every plant, and every functional unit. If no satisfactory answer is forthcoming, that activity should be redirected, scaled down, or eliminated because otherwise, the energy, time, and expense incurred is unlikely to increase transaction possibilities or success.

From analyses of responses to these three questions flow many derivative questions and, ultimately, decisions. For instance, are our customers other businesses? Government units? Individual people? In the man-made fiber manufacturing business, for instance, one's customers are both other companies, such as clothmakers, and the retail consumer, you and me. The two kinds of customers want different things and each must be satisfied. Retail customers are very much interested in the kind and characteristics of the fibers that become the clothing and other items they purchase. Trademarked, recognized name fibers are important to clothmakers and clothing manufacturers—and to the retail buyer. But the needs and wants of the three kinds of customers are not identical. The industrial customer, say a knitter, is concerned with price per pound, deliveries, and how the fibers run through the machines. The end-use customer is more concerned with the price, fit, and style of the garment. It is critical to decide who the customers really are. And, importantly, how to satisfy all of them, whether they are other organizations or different categories of individual end users.

Cadillac has introduced a new car, the Catera. It is designed to appeal to younger buyers and to those who might otherwise buy an import. Cadillac expects that a relatively large proportion of buyers will be women. As a result of these data, dealers who will sell the car are being carefully trained to deal effectively with a decidedly nontraditional Cadillac customer.

There is commonly more than a single tier or category of customer. Direct sales organizations such as Lands End or L. L. Bean are examples. It may be easier for such businesses to specify the broad categories of their customers, but it is no less important for them to thoroughly understand differentiations within their various trade categories. For instance, active hunters are more likely to value brush and briar protection than style in their clothing.

A retail car dealership may appear to have only one kind of customer, the individual new car purchaser. Often, though, car dealers sell to company fleets and police departments. They also sell used vehicles, parts, service, and financing. And there are sometimes smaller trading units within even these categories. Some dealerships sell parts solely through their service departments, while others also sell parts at retail. Deciding who the customer is may not always be obvious.

Sometimes the real question is, "What do our actual or hoped for customers truly want?" It is a question that must be asked and answered frequently by every CEO, every president, and every executive. It is an equally valid question for a law firm, local government, or hospital as it is for a church, school, or steel manufacturer.

There is only one way to know. Ask carefully. Listen even more intently, in as many ways as you can devise. Most important, use surveys and other techniques to measure, then recalibrate and measure again.

A client of ours manufactures and sells consumer products through hardware stores, electronics outlets, and large chains, such as WalMart, and the discounters, such as PACE or SAM'S CLUB. A few years ago we intensively surveyed their large customers to learn how our client and especially how its products were viewed. The executives were especially interested in customer perceptions about the *product*—its performance characteristics, price, quality, and delivery. To no one's surprise, the results showed very high acceptance of the product. No big problems there. But many large customers were not at all pleased with our client's long-used billing system. Customers said the invoices were nearly unintelligible and required considerable manual work before they could be entered into the customers' systems. No one we talked with in our client's organization had any idea that their billing process was so annoying.

Client systems and finance experts went to work. They visited and listened to customers, and they redesigned the whole system. After testing and solving the inevitable start-up problems, customers reported significantly improved overall satisfaction. An unexpected result from the new system was that the company got paid faster—

their "days outstanding" fell meaningfully. There are usually a number of benefits from finding out what the customer wants—and providing it.

Many organization groups, functions, or departments serve only, or primarily, customers inside their own firm. For instance, an aluminum casting operation may have as its sole customer the machining department in the same firm. The same three questions are entirely appropriate. If the internal customer is not being well served, if there is a more effective outside alternative, or if what is being provided is of marginal utility, then elimination, improvement, and outsourcing are alternatives.

Meeting customer desires must be a primary focus of any business strategy. The more that satisfying every customer becomes part of the company's core identity, the stronger it will be. Burger King and McDonald's, for instance, know who their customers are and have very efficient delivery mechanisms in place. Both invest heavily in trying to determine what will be wanted. Though the offerings vary over time, the cohesiveness and identity of the firm is never compromised. Taco Bell, in contrast, seems to have no core identity nor is it clear who they believe their customers are or what they want.

Assume for now that we know who our multiple customers are and we know pretty clearly just what they want. How, then, do we deliver what is wanted? Developing answers to the following questions provides the third leg of trade:

- Who are our customers?
- What do they want?
- How do we deliver?

Ultimately, someone must decide what the organization will offer to its customers and how whatever it is will be delivered. Answers to these questions determine and specify the organization's primary capabilities and its stock-in-trade. To a considerable extent, knowledge about who our customers are, together with what they want and need, can help define what might be offered. But answers to these questions do not inform about how the offerings will actually be provided or where the primary emphasis will be.

For instance, an automaker might decide to make virtually every major component in the company's own plants. Or, as in DeLorean's case, it might decide to make only a few parts, the stainless steel bodies, and purchase all others. At the extreme, the decision could be to purchase all components outside, and simply assemble the vehicles in the auto company's facilities. Such choices depend on many factors, including the company's competencies, its financial condition, available space, and so on. Often, a deciding factor is the comfort, or lack of it, that key executives experience with the various options. Another is that vertical integration is both risky and extremely expensive to establish or maintain.

A group of doctors might limit the focus of their practice to certain specialties and refer patients with different problems to other, outside, physicians. Or, the decision might be to broaden the areas of practice to encompass many specialties. Again, key factors are the ability to attract and hire people with particular competencies, partnership finances, and the owners' level of comfort with each of the possible alternatives.

## DIFFERENTIATION HELPS DEFINE IDENTITY

### Research

*Research* is clearly a major differentiation strategy in pharmaceutical, communication, electronics, and oil exploration companies, to name just four. Research, and all it implies about people, systems, and asset use, for instance, goes a long way to define the firm's identity. Research, though, takes many forms. There are the archetypical, large laboratories where scientists seek basic knowledge about the nature of things—knowledge that may have no application to trade or the firm's profits for years, if ever. The expectation of those who follow this strategy is that some percentage of laboratory or field outcomes will, someday, become available for sale. It is an expensive, long-range path that, even if only modestly successful, can provide a stream of knowledge, processes, and products available for trade decades into the future. The cost of failure, either to make the needed discoveries or to market them successfully, can be enormous. So can the benefits of success.

Just as basic, from a strategic viewpoint, are investigations into what people and organizations will be like at some distant time. An industry of futurists has developed—individuals and companies devoted to measuring what we now are, individually and collectively, and projecting what we may become in the future. Political pollsters try to predict the future "value" of candidates for elected office from measurements made months or years before the vote is taken. They are, at bottom, trying to predict the overall outcome of the trades, or trade-offs, to be made by voters in the future. Changes in wants, economic abilities, education, demographics, and many more factors are measured and examined by futurists of many kinds. This, too, is research. From it can be gleaned the kinds of products and services that will someday be in demand.

### Product or Service Development

Another strategy for enhancing trade is less concerned with discovering the basic nature of things than with changing what we already know. The goal is to add value to existing products or services. Years ago, Celanese Fibers Company had a deliberate strategy to invest modestly in pure or basic research but to aggressively expand upon the fundamental research outcomes of others, notably DuPont. There is nothing in the least unethical or improper about such a strategy. It is simply the process of adding value by revising or redesigning an existing technology, product, or service. While perhaps less risky than dependence on pure research, a product development strategy is by no means certain to add perceived value. There have been many new automobile designs based entirely on existing technology that were eventual commercial failures. Remember Packard and Studebaker? Yet, many succeed handsomely as the number of new, successful models every year demonstrates. There have been exceptions, but the major soft drink companies almost never change their basic formulas. Instead, they experiment endlessly with different variations of the same theme. Some succeed; others don't. The cost of introducing a new product is acceptable, and the possible increased business is considerable.

### Production

A third differentiation strategy is the development of great expertise and competence in *producing* a product or service. The favorable outcomes can include reduced costs, higher quality, and great delivery flexibility. If successful, sales volumes and sometimes margins are enhanced by the ability to price one's offering lower than others, thereby gaining more repeat business through customer loyalty and the ability to produce what is wanted on very short notice. Nucor Steel is a fine example of a company that has blended a product development and a production strategy to outpace its competition in the United States, Japan and elsewhere. Other examples are Mercury Marine and BIC. If the product or service is sound and in some demand, this can be a potent strategy that goes well beyond producing "things."

BIC (pens, razors, lighters) has succeeded handsomely by producing useful, inexpensive items to extraordinary levels of precision and quality. Every year, their manufacturing tolerances shrink and their products become more useful and reliable. BIC stays tightly focused on what it is and what it does best—design and manufacture high-volume, low-cost personal items of great precision and reliability.

BIC executives will seriously consider making just about any small, high-precision, low cost personal item. They don't consider building cars or making steel. Nor do they build excessively elaborate facilities or have overly complex staffs. Their systems are extraordinarily effective and constantly improved. Focus and a crisp, coherent identity are the results.

Several companies with database investigative capability now produce sound, legal research for law firms—research that would cost more and take longer if performed by lawyers at the firm. Trade is expanded for both the research company and the customer law firms through a production-driven strategy. The success of Federal Express is also grounded on a production and delivery strategy. What is "produced" is an utterly reliable, dependable service—one its customers can rely upon any time, any place.

One frequent subset of a production strategy is a concentration on *delivery* of the service or product. In recent years the two, production and delivery, have sometimes seemed to be different faces of the same strategy. The various warehouse clubs, such as SAM'S, rely on delivery or distribution of whatever the customer wants, whenever it is wanted, at the lowest possible price. Such outcomes require suppliers with highly effective production strategies in place. Together, production and delivery mean many more opportunities for trade. Electronics have greatly accelerated service delivery. Physicians in a large medical center can receive information and transmit both diagnosis and treatment suggestions to remote colleagues very rapidly indeed. This, too, is a production/delivery strategy.

### Differentiation Through High Touch and Care

Some extremely successful companies enhance trade through primary reliance on a carefully planned and conscientiously implemented high-touch strategy. The goal is to clearly demonstrate to every customer that he or she is highly valued and cared about, a key aspect of self-esteem. Leaders of such companies believe that showing high levels of personal caring counts for a lot in our increasingly technical and impersonal world. That this can be a potent strategy is shown by sales, profit, and repeat customer numbers.

Consider the retail car business. The dealer has minimal control over the cars sent by the factory. He or she can do little to enhance the product, at least in the short term. Moreover, the exact product can probably be purchased from another dealer not far away for about the same amount. So, how do you win? By providing extra value in the eyes of your customer. The most successful dealers provide a great deal of personal care—high touch. The physical surroundings, many extra services, and the behavior of every employee shows that the customer is valued. Car dealers who fully embrace this strategy have achieved published customer satisfaction ratings in the 95 percent positive range, even in years when the cars themselves were of marginal quality. Such dealers simply overwhelm product characteristics with genuine care and concern.

Piedmont Airlines was a relatively small, regional carrier prior to being acquired by U.S. Air. Piedmont's planes were never the largest, newest or fastest, nor were its fares the lowest. Yet, Piedmont enjoyed immense customer loyalty because every employee showed a personal level of caring and concern. I know a cleaning supplies company whose products are used by many manufacturing plants. Every once in a while, a manager or executive will visit a customer's plant on the late-night shift. The plant's maintenance people and supply company manager talk together about the work and how the products perform.

Guess whose products are recommended and purchased year after year even though they are more expensive?

Companies whose leaders pursue almost any differentiation approach long enough will eventually develop a sharp-edged, cohesive identity known to customers and staff alike. It can be a potent asset in the market.

### Packaging As a Differentiation Strategy

This is another primary method to enhance trade through differentiation. Packaging is much more than the design and characteristics of the container, though it is sometimes only that.

Duracell, the battery maker, developed a battery tester as part of their display container. This is added value even though the primary product itself, the battery, is the same and the tester costs little to add. Duracell does more than include the tester with its batteries. The company can package batteries in just about any number and configuration its large customers want. It will deliver on time and in ways that assure that plenty of fresh batteries are always available. All of this might be considered a successful packaging strategy. But without primary reliance on an effective production strategy, Duracell's packaging approach could not expand its volumes or profits.

Another kind of packaging is the bundling together of apparently different products and services. The intent is to increase sales for each component beyond what it could contribute alone. Truck, car, and boat dealers, for instance, offer new and used products. They also offer on-site insurance, financing, and leasing programs. Some operate profitable, specialized schools for actual and potential customers. A thoughtful packaging strategy can significantly add trade potential. Health maintenance organizations (HMOs) basically rely on a packaging strategy.

Mercury Marine Corporation (Mercury, Mariner, and Force Engines) has a primary boat-motor-trailer strategy. Mercury has long owned Bayliner and Sea Ray boat companies, among others. After listening to their dealers, it made sense to David Jones, Mercury's president, and to Chairman Jack Reichert, to develop well-designed, price-competitive packages of boats, motors, and trailers. No need to shop multiple vendors to assemble your own rig—Mercury will take care of all that. A Mercury dealer can customize your boat with Mercury engines and accessories and have you on your way with minimal trouble. Now, that is a packaging strategy grounded on longtime design and manufacturing expertise.

The following two trading strategies are important because they are so common and often have such extreme impact.

## *Acquisition/Divestiture*

There are venture capital groups, institutions, and individual investors whose primary, and even sole strategy, is to acquire and trade off entire companies and business units. In one sense they are the pattern for all traders; only the size or composition of the trade is unusual. Many have little interest in operating a company and do not intend to keep their holdings for long. As a rule, such people do not lead or have any interest in leading; rather, they barter, swap, and exchange. Their trade inventory is a portfolio of owned or controlled organizations.

Many other kinds of players and many other entities are continually involved in acquisition and divesture activities. In any trade, such as an acquisition, there is an owner, whether the owner is an individual or a larger group of shareowners. In the latter case, the owners are typically represented by a board of directors who decide whether to buy or sell company assets. It is the board whose members decide on behalf of the owners how to respond to an outside approach to buy or sell. As we have seen, much more than objective, measured value is usually considered by senior executives and board members.

Apart from the sometimes spectacular sales and swaps of entire companies, subunits and individual facilities are also offered or acquired. Specific technologies, products, processes, and licenses are also exchanged or bartered. The same questions arise: What do you want? What will you give? Why? How will the deal improve your ability to trade? The answers are extremely varied, and often transparently reasonable.

We needed the space [or manufacturing capacity or . . .].

Their product (or service) fit perfectly into our line.

It was a lot faster and took less capital to license the technology.

That division doesn't fit us anymore.

We just don't know how to run that operation. The new owners do.

I've built the (company, firm, practice, or organization) and my kids aren't interested. It's time to sell to someone with new ideas.

Certainly, buying or selling one or more productive assets is a major strategy. It can be very successful, if accompanied by strong commitment to maintaining the self-confidence of organization members. A disaster if it is not.

The Brunswick Corporation decided to get out of the defense business and put its entire defense division up for sale. The process took more than two years, a long period of anxious uncertainty for division employees. Brunswick regularly stated and then fulfilled each of its commitments to defense division people throughout the period.

Dwight Byrd, then Brunswick's general manager and now president of the Marion Composites Company, reports to new owners. He went to great lengths to maintain the self-respect of all organization members during the two-year period of great insecurity. For instance, he had the courage to commission confidential opinion and attitude surveys of all employees and, separately, of the organization's customers. He initiated significant training for all supervisory people about their new and expanded roles, and he began a thorough reexamination of the facility's reporting and control systems.

Today, the firm has no labor problems, although it is unionized. It's sales volume and profits are increasing because of a cohesive, well-understood identity people can believe in and because a far-sighted executive was determined to keep employee confidence at respectable levels despite enormous change.

### Sales, Marketing, Bidding, and Promotion

This category could readily be subdivided into at least four. Because the intent and psychology is so similar, I have elected to combine them.

Virtually every organization, profit or nonprofit, engages in sales, promotion, and marketing activities of some kind to increase trade. A much smaller number of companies have developed such activities into the long-term centerpiece of corporate strategy. Soft drink companies Coca-Cola and Pepsi, catalog retailer L. L. Bean, and housewares provider Tupperware are organizations that are driven largely by a sales strategy. To be sure, these organizations make or purchase materials, but their greatest strength is in sales and marketing. L. L. Bean does it through its often-imitated catalogues. The soft drink companies advertise and promote heavily and rely on their franchise holders to provide the face-to-face sales muscle. Tupperware is known for its sales success in small-group Tupperware parties. To this frequent traveler, it seems clear that some airlines have changed from a high-touch, customer-focused strategy to one dominated by a bewildering number of ever-changing marketing promotions and fare changes. To me, the once clear, individual characters of some carriers are changing dramatically, but I can't tell what they are trying to become.

Every organization promotes its goods and services in some way. The important issues are the proportion of the organization's resources devoted to that purpose and how high in the structure the function reports. If the senior sales executive or marketing head does not report to the president, or if only a small proportion of available funds are devoted to those activities, the organization does not, in fact, rely on a sales or marketing strategy.

Marketing and promotion take many forms. We have had a number of clients in the defense industry. In some, marketing efforts were limited to occasional top-level contacts in the DOD (Department of Defense) coupled with very costly efforts to respond fully to every RFP (request for proposal). These firms sometimes had armies of people drafting responses to projects far beyond the company's experience. A senior-level executive told me, "We're fairly small in this (defense) industry. The cheapest way to advertise ourselves is to get on every list and respond to every RFP. If we win only a few, it is worth the cost." With the reduction in defense spending, this firm can no longer afford its longtime approach to marketing and promotion and has virtually ceased operations.

Within a sales and marketing driven strategy, there are many possible variations in tactical cost and price decisions alone. To return to the retail car business, two dealers with exactly the same products may elect quite different strategies. One dealer may choose to have barely adequate facilities, a minimally competent staff, and to sell cars for a relatively low price. While the cost-price relationship produces less profit per car, he or she expects to sell more cars because of a lower price and to spend less for overhead.

A second dealer may elect to construct more appealing facilities, provide high levels of service, and to invest in selecting and training an excellent staff. His or her costs will be larger, and the volume may be less than that of a competitor. This dealer expects to be able to get a substantially higher price for each car.

A multiproduct, technology-intensive company often relies on product discovery and development. Such a firm will have made large investments in products new to the market. It may decide to price the new product sufficiently high to recover its development costs and to make a profit, in a relatively short time. At the same time, it may also have lower priced products whose development costs have long since been recovered. They can help fund the company for decades.

The true salesperson and the trader have much in common. They are practitioners of the purest form of business. An integrated sales, marketing, and promotion thrust, if well-supported and pursued over a long period, is a potent strategy for enhancing trade.

I was heartened and surprised recently to see a small plaque on the desk of a renowned biochemist in a pharmaceutical company: *Remember, nothing happens, absolutely nothing, until somebody sells something.*

### Joint Ventures

This trading strategy has become far more common in the last fifteen or twenty years. The idea is straightforward. There is some potentially profitable product or service that you and I agree will likely succeed. You have some assets such as knowledge, staff, and patents whereas I have others such as manufacturing facilities. We agree to put, say, equal amounts into developing and producing a new product. We agree to share the profits 50/50. The deal might be appealing because neither of us has all the assets needed, or we need to move quickly to market before someone else does. This joint venture is also a trade. We each give up an equally valuable "something" in the hope of getting something else that we want. Oil exploration companies may have thousands of what amount to individual joint ventures with land-owners. The companies want and are willing to pay for the right to explore on the owner's property. It is common for storeowners in a large mall to pay a percentage of their sales to the mall itself. This, too, represents a joint venture. If customers come to the mall and make purchases, both parties gain. If they don't, both lose.

There are nearly unlimited joint venture configurations. In all, a high level of shared commitment and trust is essential. It is worth noting that a lot of joint ventures don't work out well because one party comes to feel that the trade has gradually become unbalanced. It is vital in any joint venture to decide if you may want a partner— or a parent.

Most typically, there are only two partners. Sometimes there are more, and as such, the personal and interpersonal issues can become complex and bitter. It is also true that one company may have multiple joint venture partners—all in different ventures. However complex the pattern becomes, the process is still one or more trades, exchanges, or swaps. Managing the trade itself and perceptions about the trade are critical to success. I know of several joint ventures where there were three corporate partners, each of a different nationality. In only one case were the planned facilities constructed. The partnerships foundered in waves of mistrust.

## MISSIONS, VALUES, AND PURPOSES

In recent years many companies, large and small, have expended time and money to develop so-called vision or mission statements. These expensive labors are intended to yield the overarching supraordinate values, goals, and purposes toward which all important actions are to be directed.

There's probably nothing harmful in such an exercise or in the resulting lofty statement. In fact, most of them seem to sound remarkably alike, regardless of industry or specific company characteristics. Many speak of treating employees well, providing shareholders with a good return, and being good corporate citizens.

Missing from most such unarguably noble sentiments is any reality-based statement of why the place really exists. It does not exist to serve mankind or its employees. It does not exist to be the best provider of X products or Y services. It does not even exist to survive. It exists to trade profitably. That is at least a primary reason it was started, and why others have since invested time or money in it. If the organization trades profitably, it will probably survive. If it trades successfully, it can treat its people well, create new jobs, pay nice dividends, help the community, invest in research, and so on. But, first, it must trade profitably. Once that bedrock fundamental is fully understood, everything else can follow. In a remarkable number of organizations, management and people at all levels somehow ignore this absolute. Just last week I heard a radio advertisement for a huge, multinational chemical and fibers company. It said, "At [company name] good citizenship is one of our core values." What a meaningless statement and unnecessary expense. It suggests a company that has yet to achieve real strategic coherence.

Lucent Technologies is one of the independent triplets resulting from the voluntary restructuring of AT&T. Lucent's advertising strongly highlights its ownership of renowned Bell Laboratories and clearly describes its purpose as "making the things that make communication work." That is an unequivocal statement of identity. Everyone can understand what Lucent's leaders intend the company to be whether they are suppliers, customers, analysts, or employees.

Trade is the absolute. But defining it carefully takes more than a sound-bite or one-liner in a framed company pronouncement. Specifying exactly how, what, and with whom you will seek to do business defines the organization's true identity and reality. A useful purpose statement tells everyone what we are about and how everyone can contribute. In my experience, vision or purpose exercises and resulting statements add little value by themselves. When they describe a realistic, specific, and attainable state of affairs, what I've called strategic identity, such statements can be powerful guides.

## EXAMPLE

Suppose you want to manufacture and sell woodworking machines. You think it can be a successful business. You enjoy and know a lot about both woodworking and small machine design.

*Company Purpose:* To manufacture and sell machines that shape wood.

Fine. No fluff there. But not complete, either. Who will be your customers? Whom will you trade with?

We will manufacture and sell machines that shape wood to hobbyists, craftsmen, restorers, designers, and custom fabricators.

Better yet. We are *not* going to enter the industrial or mass production market. Our ultimate customers are individuals or perhaps small, custom-type shops. Odds are they have limited space and bankrolls. They will likely want great precision and long life from a relatively small number of flexible machines.

But what, exactly, will we make and sell? There is an enormous range of possible small shop wood-shaping machines, from handheld tools to those requiring fairly heavy stands and supports.

We will manufacture a limited range of best possible quality, stationary machines designed specifically for small spaces and limited capacity or thruput.

Excellent. No handheld, motorized tools. Everything stationary and space efficient. Absolutely top quality. Low volume output.

From there, it becomes straightforward to specify price ranges and other machine characteristics. At some point, we must consider how our machines will be sold. For instance, we might want to sell through distributors, mass market merchandisers, or specialty stores; or it may be better to sell direct to the customer as RBI has chosen to do. Competition, customer service, designed quality level, and other factors are also important. Many should find their way into our purpose statement.

At the conclusion of this process, everyone will be clear about what the company is truly all about. They will know the boundaries. Product characteristics, distribution, service practices, and many other issues and decisions can be readily resolved by reference to such a description. How much better is such a clear, unambiguous statement than the all too common "vision" statements that leave people bemused, confused, and sometimes incredulous. But to have genuine power, even the best statement of purpose must be lived, demonstrated, and referenced for years. A single, one-shot exercise will be soon forgotten while egregious exceptions will be long remembered.

The overriding purpose is made real and operational when a tightly conceived statement of purpose is shared with everyone, when assets, systems, people, and organization are all focused on the real goals of the organization.

A midlevel manager in a manufacturer of nuclear power plant instruments put it well:

> Around here, you will never go wrong if you decide in favor of absolute product quality. Schedules, costs, labor problems, and even deliveries all come after quality. Every employee knows that, from day one. You will never get in trouble by demanding absolute quality at every step.

That's the result of a clearly understood purpose and, more important, a shared congruence of belief and expectation. Such coherence is a major company advantage that is visible to employees and customers alike. It can guide the real decisions that determine the firm's ability to succeed.

Chapter 4

# Models and Fads

Since World War II an array of management techniques and models have been introduced. A few have already been mentioned or discussed and many more are part of the common language and mental toolkits of executives everywhere. Virtually all have proven to be effective in some situations and not so successful in others. At one time or another, some have reached the status of fad—almost of sacred mantras. Say it often enough and things will get better. Pour enough funds into "Method A" or "Procedure Q" and success is assured. Leaders are as susceptible to fads as anyone else.

Though relatively few executives realize it, the best of these conceptions have steadily evolved and improved through years of practice and research. Indeed, they tend to recycle every decade or so, though under new names, with better supporting data and different sponsors. We can usually rely on the carefully tailored application of such models to improve the effectiveness of most organizations.

Winning approaches, those most likely to work in practice, have in common that they engage and encompass the primary clusters and key linkages described in this book. Conversely, techniques that concentrate on making changes within just a single cluster of factors and that ignore the others are not likely to succeed. Many costly systems have been designed that had no connection to either employee commitment or to customer satisfaction. Not surprisingly, installation has usually produced disappointing results.

When systems provide relevant information and organization processes allow people greater decision-making influence and control over the work environment, the results are usually gratifying. Add systems that financially reward measured achievement, appropriate training, and customer input about what they want, and you have a crisp company identity and a recipe for real success. It all depends on focused, energetic, and above all persistent leadership, not on any single technique however appealing it may be.

For instance, job enrichment and self-managed groups are both ways to move real power and decision-making authority down the organization ladder to people much closer to the work itself. Together or singly, both represent real employee empowerment and are often successful because they meet basic human needs for self-respect. Many times I have seen such promising approaches deliver much less than they might because management would not, or could not, redesign the compensation system to reward the achievements that were the goals in the first place.

In the same way, a new organization structure, that actively and deliberately promotes key employee confidence and that is also designed to crisply focus on meeting internal and external customer needs, will likely succeed. The same is true for changes in people and asset use. Initiatives undertaken in relative isolation from customer and key employee needs will rarely succeed. Link all three groups of primary factors and you can energize and redirect even very large companies.

The following list supplies a sample of some currently prominent management models and also their progenitors of the past four or five decades. Each approach gained adherents and was implemented initially because it was consistent with developing executive belief, style, and philosophy, and because it projected improved business performance. Many of the earliest approaches were, at the time, very innovative and even revolutionary. It is a tribute to their creators and to visionary leaders in research and practice that a high proportion are imbedded in the processes and identities of so many successful companies.

In the following list, eight categories of leader purposes, beliefs, and intentions are given in bold type. Under each category are some important related models and operational methods.

1. *Provide people with knowledge and skill so they can contribute.*

- Mechanisms to regularly communicate with people such as videos, newsletters, e-mail, meetings, etc.
- Training and education programs

- Performance appraisals
- Management development and mentoring
- Cross-training, rotation, career planning
- Job posting
- Customer visits
- Vestibule training
- 360° Feedback

2. *Give people real power and authority and they will contribute.*

- Teams and task forces
- Self-managed work groups
- Work enrichment
- Employee survey-feedback processes
- Internal advisory boards
- Quality circles
- Delayering: empowering
- Motivator-hygiene theory: building in motivators
- Decentralization: pushing power out and down

3. *Properly used, money will focus energy and shape behavior toward greater contribution.*

- Piecework pay
- Spot bonuses
- Gainsharing plans/Incentive plans
- Profit sharing
- Team-based compensation
- Stock ownership

4. *Open, candid work climates and caring relationships in the context of work will yield responsiveness, satisfaction, and higher contribution.*

- T groups/sensitivity training
- Benefit plans
- Culture change
- Learning organizations
- The Managerial Grid; 9,9 management style

- Theory Y management
- Creativity/innovation training
- Counseling

5. *Get the very best people and they will contribute.*

- Validated selection: tests, bio data, assessment centers, honesty tests, job sample, lie detectors, etc.
- Interview training and methods: individual, group; peers, subordinates, superiors; psychological
- Background verification and vetting
- Career and succession planning
- Diversity
- Human resource information systems: data banks of employee desires, skills, and work histories.

6. *When everyone fully understands what is important and expected of them, they will contribute more.*

- Mission statements
- Core values descriptions
- Position descriptions
- Role clarification processes
- Visioning
- Organization development
- Alternate channels/ombudsman
- Management by objectives (MBO)

7. *The right product and service delivery processes, systems, and measurements will allow us to steadily improve customer satisfaction.*

-                   Zero defects/defects per unit
- Statistical quality/process control
- Systems analysis and Industrial engineering
- Operations research
- Customer satisfaction measures
- Total quality, ISO, Baldridge, Six Sigma
- Ergonomics/workplace and equipment design

- JIT (just in time)
- Continuous improvement; Kaisen
- Cycle time reduction
- Activity-based accounting
- Benchmarking

8. *Efficient internal work processes and better systems of all kinds will let us do more with a lot fewer people.*

- Business process reengineering
- Downsizing/rightsizing/delayering
- Outsourcing of functions
- Restructuring
- Centralizing/decentralizing
- Process mapping

Understanding usually grows slowly and rarely smoothly: every innovator and each new management model is grounded on knowledge previously accumulated by many others. So, it should not surprise us that some useful early formulations reappear years later—refined, changed and renamed. Typically, the earliest expressions of any new management conception sketch a system of key factors, fundamental connections, possible applications, and expected outcomes. Subsequent research and practice will inevitably refine and improve—and sometimes discard—earlier formulations.

People who practiced business systems analysis and industrial engineering in the 1950s, and there were many, studied and improved business processes and procedures in thousands of manufacturing plants, offices, and laboratories. Their primary tools were keen observation and, most important, the active help of people actually doing the work. Such analysts had no computers— maybe a noisy, thirty pound, desk-filling calculator. The most accomplished analysts I knew were adept at stimulating and developing creative improvement ideas from people on the job. What these analysts did is not so different from what today might be called "process mapping" and "cycle time reduction" or even "continuous improvement" and sometimes even "empowerment." Some aspects of what we call today "business process reengineering" is in the same tradition. Except, those old-fashioned business systems analysts and industrial engineers often defined the problems they faced, the techniques they used, and the solutions they proposed much more broadly because they tended to be longtime employees who thoroughly understood the business, its people, and its identity. And, they often used a variety of creative techniques to gain the confidence of workers in the service of greater process efficiency and reliability. For instance, I saw an early, unnamed version of quality circles regularly used in a river transportation company in the 1950s. Interestingly, each tow boat's crew was, in fact, a largely self-managed work group. The prevailing labor relations climate was such that each crew even within the same company could vote to gain or reject union membership. Most stayed out.

Measurement has always been part of business and of manufacturing. Forty years ago "statistical quality control" (or SQC) and "zero defects" were watchwords, especially in defense manufacturing where a single defect could have catastrophic consequences. But SQC was soon applied to a broad range of products. SPC or "statistical process control" emerged as a way of keeping key processes, not just products, on track. Today very similar models are used in TQM (total quality management), ISO certification, and Baldridge Award preparation. The handbooks, rules, and prescribed procedures for each of these successful approaches are dominated by many specific references to how people must be involved, trained, and encouraged in order for the particular quality improvement model to work. The core objective of these models is, of course, better product and service quality delivered to the customer. They usually work because they fit and help enrich the firm's strategic identity. They promote employee self-confidence, and they focus on satisfying inside and outside customers.

Top-notch leaders don't have to be brilliant, but all I have known are very smart. Smart enough, certainly, to know that business performance ultimately depends on the kinds of people hired and on how they are treated at work. The human relations movement began well before World War II, as did an emphasis on developing scientifically sound tests and other techniques to select people who were likely to perform well. Bio data, in the form of weighted application blanks and, in the 1960s, assessment centers, attracted much research interest as have various interview methods. In improved form, all of these selection systems remain in use because smart leaders knew then and know now that successful trade requires the devoted energy of skilled, talented people, even though "people costs" on the balance sheet may be a relatively small proportion of the total cost of goods sold.

The human relations movement gradually matured and came to encompass virtually every conceivable way to train and communicate with employees and, increasingly, with customers.

Incentive pay plans, management by objectives, and performance appraisals remain key approaches to defining individual goals and linking them to corporate objectives. But such approaches must be regularly redesigned to meet new realities. Years of corporate realignments and restructurings have thrown a lot of company objectives, and even identities, into question and sometimes chaos, at least as experienced by people who work in such firms.

One longtime manager in a twice-sold, three times reorganized company told me recently:

> Hell, I don't know what is wanted any more. I don't even know who we are these days. So, I just focus on week-by-week plant results that seem reasonable. How can I reassure myself, let alone my people?

Partly because so many firms have lost their once strong sense of cohesion, purpose, and identity, leaders have increasingly become interested in re-creating and clarifying for everyone compan} purposes, missions, and values. As discussed earlier, developing mission statements and "visioning" are two current approaches to solving an old problem—who and what are we as a company?

Theory Y is the human relations notion that under the right conditions people can and will learn to work effectively on their own in the service of worthwhile objectives. It evolved into the Managerial Grid and both became important topic areas in thousands of management training programs. Employee and customer opinion surveys greatly improved and became preferred tools to inform and more tightly bind parts of the organization together, and to connect the organization directly with its customers. Work enrichment has become so much a part of good management practice in many organizations that today the term is rarely used or even recognized by newer managers. Enrichment basically means empowering people to make important choices and decisions about their work. Enrichment and empowerment are at the center of today's total quality management and self-managed work group initiatives.

I hope that this brief and admittedly subjective review convinces you that when it comes to business leadership there is very little entirely new under the sun. Beware fads and nostrums from any source. Most of the approaches in the list above remain useful. Most can help improve business performance, but only if they are carefully tailored to the particular organization *and* are diligently supported and pursued for some years.

I hope, too, that the foregoing discussion shows that the best management concepts constantly evolve; in some form, they hold up in practice over many years and across many industries. Each remains both popular and powerful because it encompasses far more than just a change or two in company organization, people, or systems. Fully embraced at all levels and resourced by leaders for some years, such methodologies can become so accepted that the firm's climate and even its core identity may change.

Certainly, a new system or other new initiative may be the initial driver of desired improvement. But if investment in architecture-level change (i.e., people, organization, assets, and systems) is to succeed, if it is to add long-term trading muscle, it must fully encompass and support employee needs for self-respect and confidence. Ultimately, it should aim to better satisfy the organization's customers. Every truly successful leadership model I have seen in use has largely met those difficult standards.

It also seems true that a single technique that considers only customer or employee satisfaction without impacting company systems or asset use, for examples, will not have lasting influence. We once briefly had a client whose executives went to great lengths, and no little expense, to develop sophisticated measurement systems intended to discover what it would take to fully satisfy each primary industrial customer—what customer executives wanted, needed and hoped for from their supplier. What, it turned out, that the customers really wanted was a much higher quality, more reliable product but at about the same cost. They said "Others in the market are doing it, so why don't you?

Despite previous commitments and assurances, our client executives were not willing to "turn the damn ship upside down." They felt that their long history and close, personal relationships with customer executives would guarantee customers for their existing product. They were wrong. Their market share has fallen from 42 percent to 28 percent in just six years because the leaders were not willing to commit the assets, add the systems, or change the organization.

There is current interest in so-called "broadbanding" of salary ranges. From what I've seen, few such plans have much connection to, or influence on, the other architectural elements, on employee sense of self-worth, or on customer satisfaction. Yes, compressing twenty or thirty salary grades into six or eight, each with a wider salary range will modestly change the compensation system. But in no case I've examined is there any linkage that explains how employee or customer needs are to be better met because of the change. Nor does the reduced number of salary ranges flow from a reconsideration of the use of company assets, its people, or the way the place should work. Absent such vital linkages, "broadbanding" usually seems to be a project without a purpose and is unlikely to add anything to the economic (trading) clout of the company.

Currently, "business process reengineering" (BPE) usually describes a major work process and system redesign initiative intended to reduce costs, cut cycle times, and provide better information. Whatever else they may do, large BPE efforts vacuum up large assets. Such projects also dramatically alter the number of people and positions, and sometimes organization structure. But BPE is rarely instituted with much commitment to employee involvement or participation. There is little evident regard for continued employee commitment or for satisfying customers better. BPE projects are typically said by employees to be thinly disguised staff reduction efforts that fool no one for very long. Because these often enormously costly projects do not encompass all three major components, they are unlikely to accomplish much more than some work simplification and temporary cost reduction through layoff.

Any well-considered change initiative is likely to succeed if it deliberately includes all three component groups and their primary linkages. Under such requirements, many of the methodologies listed earlier in this chapter can be artfully blended to yield very satisfying outcomes. But they must be blended because under even ideal circumstances, no single change model has the "reach" and power needed.

True culture change, one that fundamentally alters the traditional ways of believing and acting, always engages a variety of models to link all three groups of driving forces, company identity, people, and customers. A strategy aimed at causing lasting culture change will alter, usually several times, the firm's people, systems, and ways of operating. Culture change is enormously difficult. In large organizations, a decade or more of persistent work may be needed, in smaller companies, at least a few years. Although an all-encompassing, culture-level change will usually take years, dramatic improvements can be achieved in much less time with careful planning, a blended approach, and the persistent, energetic support of organization leaders.

Entrepreneurs and smaller company executives have marvelous opportunities to conceive and create their vision of a desirable, affordable organization. Ken Iverson did it with Nucor Steel, Ray Hunt with Hunt Consolidated, Tom Davis with Piedmont Airlines and many others. Such leaders can choose from a menu of evolving and improving management models and formulas to develop an organization that embodies their conceptions. My advice to such leaders has often been to attend at least as closely to building a strong, well-conceived, and crisply focused organization identity as to professional, technological, and financial matters substantially changing deeply imbedded organization styles and values later on is so difficult—as a great many second and later generation leaders have discovered.

# SECTION II:
## STRATEGIC IDENTITY
## AND
## THE FOUR LEVERS OF CHANGE

FIGURE 3. The Role of Strategic Identity in Trade

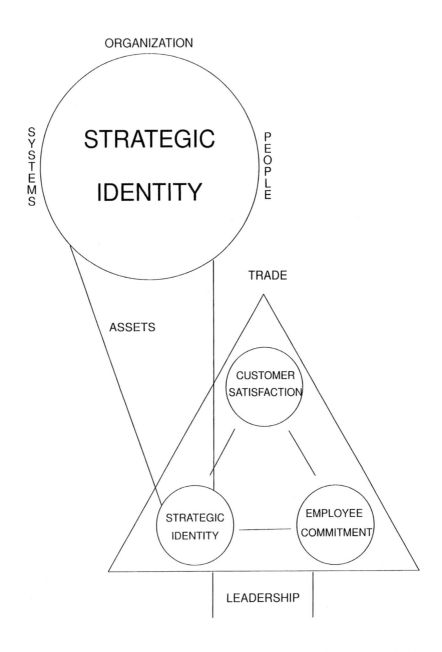

*The firm, the enduring, the simple and the modest are near to virtue.*

—Confucius

Strategic identity is the soul of the enterprise, its purpose, meaning, and actual strategy-in-use as understood and experienced by members and outside observers.

One of the primary requirements and major personal frustrations that confronts nearly every top-level, decision-making leader is determining how to effectively project his or her vision, decision, and power throughout the organization. The larger and more diverse the organization, the more difficult the problem. As a practical matter, top executives of large companies can directly and personally influence only a few other people in the organization, such as board members, direct reports, and perhaps key function or division leaders. An executive's personal impact and influence diffuses and becomes blurred more readily than most would like to believe. Time, distance, and the press of other responsibilities preclude a greater personal reach into the organization and to its individual members. Certainly, site visits and other events allow the executive leader to be seen but are not, in fact, very useful conduits for projecting real influence. Company publications, e-mail, and other techniques can allow a leader to describe and explain, but they cannot demonstrate and prove to sometimes cynical, fearful people.

Top executive leaders have available four practical tools—as illustrated in the preceding figure—that can successfully project their intentions and expectations throughout the organization and beyond. They alone can provide the real traction leaders need, especially in times of uncertainty and change. These are the enduring elements that are inherent characteristics of every business organization. Change any one of them, and the organization will change. These built-in elements are the always present architectural features of any firm; they are also the potentially pivotal levers of change, of tightened focus, or redirection.

Apart from the actual intent and meaning of any particular top-level action about organization, systems, asset use, or staff, these four features are highly visible and very closely observed by most employees. A change in any will be known widely and very quickly because it is real, and it is now. It will be far more broadly observed, discussed, and interpreted than most senior executives anticipate. Change in one or more of the four characteristics will be read by employees at all levels as projections of top, executive authority and, most important, of future intention and expectation. What senior leaders actually *do* in each category is vital. What such actions say to employees, customers, and other constituents is just as important.

I have been in offices, laboratories, and manufacturing plants when the shop floor grapevine carried the word that a remote corporate-level vice president was to be sacked, or a facility was to be bought or sold, or a big lay-off would soon be announced. More often than not, the informal communication net got the message mostly right. As the word spread, especially if confirmed, groups of hourly people, professionals, and managers began to huddle here and there. Within hours a consensus usually emerged about what it all meant for the future. In times of uncertainty, people need each other to help build or rebuild a sense of meaning and integration. Informal social contacts provide that opportunity.

I am sure from many conversations that few CEOs realize just how closely their every move is observed, interpreted, and projected into the future, and not only by employees. Customers, analysts, and suppliers, too, are often close observers. The most visible and personally relevant changes in any company usually concern the following:

- What is done with assets
- The organization's configuration and power distribution
- Major system changes and what they mean to individuals
- The acquisition, departure, positioning, and movement of people

Alterations in one or more of these four architectural features receive the high attention they do because, taken together, they form the core of the company—they define the place for its members and others. When one or more element is changed significantly, the meaning and identity of the firm become something different, at least somewhat. It follows that a leader determined to alter, reenergize, or redirect a company should focus on deliberately converting the architectural features into levers of change. First, because they are already or can readily be brought within the leader's reach and personal influence. Second, because they are the most reliable tools leaders have for changing, developing, and refocusing the firm's identity and meaning into something different. And, third, because they are already visible and of great interest.

Any firm's strategic identity, then, is a blending of four components in ways unique to itself and the ideas of its leader(s). As experienced by employees and observed by outsiders such as customers, analysts, and suppliers, a firm's identity *is* its present and reasonably probable future thrust and direction. It is the expression of values, purposes, and intentions along with actual and potential competencies, and reputation. Most important, it is a more or less consistent and coherent sense of integrated wholeness projected into the future. For employees and others, it can be the "reason to believe" in the future of the enterprise. Strategic coherence and strategy are not necessarily the same. Some executive leadership groups spend a great deal of time and money developing elaborately detailed plans and strategies. Such plans will become part of the firm's strategic coherence, its identity, only if assets, systems, people, and the organization itself are altered, committed, and directed to that purpose. Saying it is so does not make it so, as the number of elegant but unused strategic plans attest. The process of creating an appealing strategy document is a lot easier than implementing and successfully integrating a different mission or purpose. The success of a significantly new strategy can be judged by the extent to which it becomes an accepted part of the core identity of the firm—its strategic coherence. Real strategic change takes years.

At a practical level, unless company disaster looms near, it is generally most effective to dispassionately decide and concentrate on just one or two of the four factors, those that seem to be the principle barriers to successful trade. Make the necessary changes and intensively communicate them to every employee. Clearly specify the reason, purpose, intention, and expectations associated with each change. Show how each will realistically impact associated employees at multiple levels and in multiple functions. Be as honest and forthright as you can legally be. *Remember:* The four components are avidly watched billboards to employees and customers.

In time, all human institutions tend to lose their basic character. In business, this process is typically accompanied by reduced differentiation in the eyes of customers and slackened commitment from employees. Firms that have remained successful for a very long time have usually had leaders who understood how to regularly reinvent and reenergize the company. They have used the four levers to regain employee focus and confidence and to reestablish a crisp, differentiating share-of-mind with their customers.

Leadership cannot be understood apart from context. Leaders are, of course, made visible and empowered by their titles and positions. But they are defined by what they do, where and when they do it, and by the outcomes. These, after all, are what matter to owner-investors, customers, and employees.

Presidents and CEOs are much more constrained, and their actions are more shaped by circumstances than is often believed. The basic identity and character of the company define the fence line, the boundaries within which the chief executive can operate with reasonable assurance. Except in fairly new or small firms, the available assets, people, systems, and the organization itself can all be formidable restraints on leader intentions.

Many characteristics of people in leadership positions have been measured and catalogued. We know a lot about their educational and family backgrounds, styles, personalities, intelligence, and even physical attributes. But these factors, together or singly, have not proven to be very helpful in predicting success. We may know about individual *leaders,* but we know much less about the process and practice of *leadership.* The art of leadership is a complex interaction among personal attributes, the power of position and the unique characteristics of the company. The truly accomplished leader is effective mostly because of what he or she believes and actually does with the four tools available—the architectural components of every firm.

# Chapter 5

# Assets

The characteristics and deployment of a firm's assets, together with how they are valued, shows the kind of identity the company is likely to have, or its leaders to desire for it. In turn, that can signal the specific differentiation approaches most likely to be used. Assets come in many forms and vary greatly in utility and value over time. Here, I very briefly suggest some of the main kinds of assets and how they relate to company identity and leader intentions.

Perhaps the most obvious assets are financial. "Cash on hand and in banks" is how one line of my firm's financial report reads. While cash may be the most accessible financial asset, it is far from the only one. Other assets include the company's invested funds, its work in process, other inventories, receivables, and reserves. The ability to raise funds by borrowing or by issuing more stock is also an asset. A lot of people carefully watch what happens to these assets for clues about the company's strength and its leaders' future intentions. So, by the way, do substantial numbers of employees. From my observation, a considerably larger proportion of employees at all levels are more financially interested and astute than, say, twenty years ago.

Another form of asset is land. Apart from the land under a manufacturing plant or office, which may be leased or owned, many large companies own staggering amounts of other real estate. Energy companies, for instance, own leases on thousands of parcels. One relevant question is whether the company's landholdings are likely to be used to generate or facilitate exchanges in its primary lines of business.

For oil exploration firms or those involved in rail transportation, mining, paper, or development, for examples, large landholdings usually make sense. They are at least potentially productive assets and are consistent with such firms' business purposes. Many companies, though, have substantial wealth invested in land that has no discernable relationship to the firm's purpose or identity. With the frequent acquisitions and divestitures of recent years, many companies now have major land and other holdings they don't really want because the properties were acquired as part of other deals. When the value of such "accidental" land assets begins to distract and absorb leader attention, it may signal a major shift in direction. I once knew a man who owned a number of profitable, well-located franchises acquired years before. He suddenly realized that he was really in the real estate, not the fast-food, business. That revelation drove a dramatic restructuring of the whole enterprise.

Plants, offices, laboratories, and equipment are other kinds of assets. Once again, an important question is whether and to what extent these assets are used to advance the primary trading purposes of the company. Are such expensive facilities sited and designed to add real muscle or not? A gaming company's elaborate facilities in Las Vegas or Atlantic City are critical to its differentiation strategy. Stockholders, analysts, and employees are likely to see such investments as "right" for the enterprise and supportive of its central purposes. The same kinds of assets would seem wildly incoherent if held by many other kinds of companies. A communications company we work with once had dozens of very attractive, expensive offices around the country—all leased by a remote group at corporate headquarters. When the leaders restructured the company into true profit and loss centers, on-site managers quickly moved to much less costly offices.

The age and condition of equipment is often another signal of future intention. Some years ago an associate and I had an engagement in a large manufacturing facility, one of many owned by the client company. After a few hours, Hugh looked at me and said without much expression:

> This place is going to be closed or sold, I'd bet within a year or two. These people are busting their humps, but it isn't going to make any difference.

From my own observation, I had to agree. The equipment was old and there were frequent breakdowns. Employees had creatively and almost frantically fashioned all kinds of temporary repairs from whatever parts they could scrounge. Many were using small tools brought from home and were even buying small parts on their own from a local hardware store. Despite some optimistic management statements, a few of the hardworking employees suspected the truth but hoped that by extra effort they could somehow save the plant and their jobs. We called our primary contact, the corporate vice president of personnel, and described our impressions. He didn't know, but promised to find out. It didn't make much sense for us or the client to embark on a long-term assignment if our perceptions and projections were accurate. They were. The assignment was mutually canceled and the plant closed within the year.

Conversely, a clean facility and the addition or upgrading of equipment sends a positive signal to employees and visitors. The addition of assets is congruent with at least maintaining the facility's position in the company's overall plans. People look for fit, for consistency and congruence of management actions and statements. When they find it, their self-confidence improves noticeably.

There are also real, if less tangible, assets that wise leaders build, husband, and protect. Some are important to achieving long-term differentiation and identity. For instance, a firm's reputation*s* (there are always more than one) with its employees, owners, and customers. Car dealer Sewell has achieved a national reputation for exemplary service and a lot of satisfied, repeat customers, even though the cars he sells are exactly the same as those sold by other dealers. Software provider Broadway & Seymour is building a powerful reputation in the banking industry. Like many assets, a positive reputation usually takes years to build. In contrast, because it is the umbrella for Bell Laboratories and Western Electric, both long-trusted names, Lucent Technologies will have instant reputation despite a new name. A strongly positive reputation, or good will, can clearly differentiate one firm from another and as such has real value. The marketplace puts a value on goodwill and reputation, especially when a firm is sold or its leaders want to borrow funds. Potential customers often begin by probing a supplier's reputation, as do many potential employees.

A positive, long-term reputation is most often a potent asset, but there can be drawbacks when the leadership is determined to change the firm's basic identity. In the minds of many, reputation can become much like an unspoken, unwritten contract. Employees, customers, and suppliers often believe and behave as though the reputation *is*, in fact, an agreement. Change the way the firm acts toward any constituency, and that group is likely to feel that an important agreement has been violated. As a Piedmont Airlines captain said to me after the acquisition by U.S. Air in 1989:

> For years, Piedmont was known in the industry as a captain's airline with the best people in the business. We had top execs who knew the company inside and out. We were a personal and personable outfit. None of that is true anymore.

What a firm's people know and can do is certainly an asset, as is more tangible evidence of innovation such as patents. Like plants and equipment, knowledge and skills will deteriorate unless regularly and deliberately upgraded through planned work experiences, training, and education. Although usually a mistake, the training budget is typically the first to be cut during any retrenchment. General Electric is especially noted for maintaining a large and effective technical training effort in both strong and weaker times. GE obviously values its technical employees. Any sudden or substantial reduction in such training will be taken by many technical employees as a signal that their skills are less valued than before. One result could easily be more decisions to leave the company.

Reputation can be deliberately created to become a primary differentrating asset. When he took over as President and CEO of Cogna Systems Corporation, Jim Van Wagenen faced 20 percent annual turnover of the systems programming people, whose output was the backbone of the company. Because of the high turnover of talented staff in an admittedly very competitive market, recruiting costs were large. More important, customers were regularly disappointed and dissatisfied.

Van Wagenen determined to differentiate Cogna from other systems houses by fully satisfying every customer. This he proposed to do by deliberately recreating the entire organization in ways that would improve employee confidence and self-esteem. It took several years, but in the end, unplanned turnover was 4 percent, and 90 percent of Cogna's customers said they were fully satisfied.

Recruiting costs and delays fell to almost zero as Cogna became known in the systems community as the place to work—if you could get in.

Relationships, licenses, contracts, and other agreements such as property and equipment leases can be primary assets. A contract to market a hot product or a license to manufacture it can be valuable. A neighbor of mine has become wealthy by leasing properties with options to buy, which he exercises when the market is suitable. You've got to take some losses, but a variety of agreements can still become assets.

Ownership of the names of well-known products or services provides another vehicle for differentiation. Product names such as Kleenex and Worcestershires sauce are so well-known that they have passed from owned trade name status to common use. Few trade names ever achieve that fame, of course because most are vigorously protected and guarded by their owners, just as they would any other valuable asset. Especially in the last ten or twenty years, many product names have been purchased without acquisition of the previously attached manufacturing assets. A well-established product name brings with it almost immediate differentiation. Simply acquiring established names can, however, signal a failure to bring to market products of one's own.

The meaning of a change in assets or asset deployment is not always clear but is nearly always important to understanding what kind of strategic identity and character a firm's leaders are trying to achieve. As one major league investor put it, *"Just watch the assets."* It's good advice.

How and where assets are acquired and used is an important and visible part of a firm's meaning. Employees, customers, and others look to the congruence of asset-focused actions for clues about how their self-interests will be affected in the future. Change in the deployment of significant assets often signals a change in leader intentions.

# Chapter 6

# Organization

*Organization* is one of four primary vehicles for getting things done. It links the actions of people with multiple assets in the service of some more-or-less shared, understood, and coherent intent. The linkages among people and to the assets are accomplished by systems of enormous variety.

The bedrock reason for a business organization to exist is to transform assets into resources for the purpose of trading with some other entity. Asset transformation and subsequent trades are brought about by the actions of people who choose to come together in some way for the purpose. The "in some way" modifier recognizes that tribe members chipping stone implements for trade in the mouth of their home cave may, today, be people working together but linked by computers in a so-called "virtual" organization. So long as people are linked together in a common and agreed purpose as described above, there's nothing necessarily "virtual" about such organizations. They can be entirely real to the people involved. What is important is that people care about the success of the company, not where they work.

Transforming assets and trading the outcomes to others usually involves many steps and processes, from research and development through billing and accounts receivable. Each specification, each process and procedure, each input and output represents systems that bind the organization together so that its members can efficiently go about transforming assets into trade. First, there must be an organization of some kind.

One factor over which leaders can exercise much control is the structure and shape of the organization—much control, but not complete control. Organizations of any size usually have a shadow or informal structure that can be very different from that shown on the official organization charts, or from that believed to exist by the top executives. The informal organization structure, together with the network of communications, influences, roles, and norms, can support or seriously restrict executive authority and desires. Informal, invisible structures can be just as powerful within the board of directors as in any plant or office. We regularly read about the firing of a shocked senior executive who had little idea that such potent opposition even existed. Many years ago as a first-level supervisor, I was often transferred among my employer's manufacturing and laboratory locations. Only once did I first learn of a transfer through the formal chain of command.

Professional and trade group memberships, shared interests, and previous school and work associations, coupled with extraordinary communication alternatives, enable shadow organizations to readily cross organization boundaries. On occasion, I have seen the influence of such informal, across-company associations guide and change the impact of executive decisions.

An organization's structure always encompasses many elements and relationships, only a few of which are clearly and officially defined. Some are assumed and rarely questioned. For instance, two soft drink bottling plants with common ownership will probably have identical formal reporting structures, titles, procedures, and roles. In one, people regularly go to anyone, at any level, to get help and decision. In another, the chain of command is expected to be rigidly followed, and woe to anyone who does not. In one plant I know of, breaking the very detailed manufacturing division instructions for a sensible reason is tolerated, expected, and even rewarded. In a sister plant, the same behavior is strictly prohibited.

Many large, publically held companies have long had a large board of directors, a chief executive officer (CEO), a president, and a chief operating officer (COO). Equally large private companies can typically meet the legal requirements with a very small board, and usually do. Often, too, the roles of CEO, president, and COO are combined in one person. Final accountability for results is obvious in such private concerns; it is much more diffuse and unclear in many large, public companies. Should it be? Is the assumed best structure really helpful? Structure should support and facilitate achievement; it should be deliberately designed to facilitate trade. If it does not demonstrably do so, the structure should be changed. As a rule, simpler is better.

Wholly unsupported assumptions sometimes drive the addition of new management levels to the organization pyramid. Prime among these assumptions is the curious idea that a person can effectively supervise, direct, and guide only some specific number of subordinates. I am aware of no credible evidence that supports such an assumption. Much more important than the number of subordinates are their skills, motivation, maturity, similarity of function, and geographic dispersal. Competent first-level factory supervisors can often quite effectively supervise forty or fifty people if their functions are similar, their skills reasonable, and if they are clustered within a single field of view and access. If any of these conditions is not the case, fifteen or twenty might be the maximum reasonable span of control for the same supervisor.

Many senior-level executives have confidently asserted to me that management spans of control should never exceed some number, usually six or seven. When asked, none has been able to provide me with a source for their belief. It appears to be a piece of folklore passed from one manager to another. An effective span of control depends on the needs and nature of the organization and on the characteristics of both the supervisor and the supervised. There is no reliable rule of thumb.

To effectively support trade and its enabling strategies, an organization's structure should reflect and describe desired relationships among individuals, groups, functions, and larger organization units—including, especially, customers. The fundamental purpose for describing such relationships is to clarify as many expectations as possible. People need to know what to personally expect from each other, and as they are members of organization units. DuPont-Merck, a joint venture, is a nearly new but quite substantial worldwide pharmaceutical company. After only a year or two of operation, company executives decided to focus intensively on increasing the contribution of the large human resource (HR) function throughout the world. Information from HR's internal "customers" was used to help redesign the entire department. Leading companies known for expertise in HR matters were contacted to see how they defined and achieved HR success—so called "benchmarking." Virtually all DuPont-Merck HR managers were collaboratively involved with senior leaders in the restructuring and redesign of their own function. Along with a new structure, most key roles were redefined and assets such as people, systems, and budgets were allocated to better satisfy HR's internal customers.

Among the lessons from many restructurings are that flat organizations are often more effective than tall, and more unit autonomy is frequently better than less. Often, but not always. Even so, the shape and dimensions of an organization's structure are less critical than the expectations it establishes and clarifies for its members.

We have worked with some clients whose executives have taken the idea of function and unit autonomy to extremes. It has not, generally, been successful. One, for instance, declared that just about every internal function was a "business unit." Human resources, accounting, advertising, advanced research, and many others were designated "business units" and so depicted on the organization chart.

This bizarre structure was strongly recommended by one of the giant consulting firms. Clearly, these advisors did not understand this single technology company, its culture, or its commercial environment. Because there was no demonstrable advantage to trade, the new structure was received with derision. After only a year, internal conflicts have increased among functions and departments. Cooperation has declined, and there are palpable walls between groups. Transfer costs are increasing rapidly, and innovation is on the decline. Why? Because groups without clear and measurable impacts on trade will look for something else to confer and validate self-importance. Most of the departments, suddenly called business units, do not visibly or measurably impact trade. Unless there is a willingness to install and support extremely costly internal and external measurements and transfer payment systems, few internal departments can produce anything like a balance sheet. They are not "business units," however useful and even essential their contribution. This is one of many examples of executives persuaded into implementing a fad completely at odds with the reality of the organization. The executives lost their focus on the customer and on trade.

Have you noticed a cycle in these kinds of activities? Does it seem to you that, for a time, centralizing almost every function is the agreed best way? Then, some years later, a decentralizing wave appears to gather broad support? You are correct, such cycles have happened several times before, and at their peak, each position becomes accepted management wisdom.

Excesses then begin to appear and, gradually, a revision sets in, and the cycle begins to repeat. Fads and recycled approaches are doubtless profitable for consulting firms, if not always for their clients. The lesson for us all is to beware accepted or faddish solutions, regardless of the status of their sources or proponents. Instead, focus and design the organization's structure to foster trade and demonstrably support a coherent identity. Design structure to help.

If part of a particular approach to improving trade includes modifying how some people act and what they do, then a primary tool is the organization's structure. Training for the purpose of altering people's attitudes and behavior is not nearly so effective as changing or defining what is expected on the job. Change what people expect, and what is expected of them, and their actions will change. So, eventually, will their attitudes.

A carefully designed organization should be accompanied by defined expectations for individuals and groups. This is what the notion of individual and organization role is all about, and why it is so important. What we think our role is determines, in large measure, how we act. That is just as true for a CEO or a lawyer, as it is for a company manager. In my experience, an organization chart laced with dotted authority lines usually breeds indecision and discomfort. Yes, such structures can create an illusion of oversight and safety, since any important action requires much consultation and agreement. Under conditions of nearly continuous change in both risk and opportunity, conditions most companies confront today, delay and upward delegation to avoid blame can be very costly.

An organization's structure should also communicate clearly about its purposes and the kinds of trades that its leaders hope to make. When any structure is burdensome, unclear, or confusing, so will be an organization's purpose and coherence. That is sometimes one of the problems associated with corporate staffs. People in cohesive operating units, such as plants or divisions, often do not see much connection between corporate activities and roles and the real purpose of the organization. In such cases, the basic or corporate structures and role definitions are likely at fault.

The goal of structure, then, is to sharpen and clarify expectations to help support various trade-enhancing approaches and the basic character of the place.

When a requirement to respond to genuine, tectonic-plate level change becomes evident to an organization's leaders, changing the structure and the roles of people are often the most expeditious responses available. There is probably no faster way to broadly demonstrate and communicate a change in fundamental intention, thrust, and direction.

## *MATRIX STRUCTURES*

Matrix structures are among those supposed palliatives that seem to periodically rise and decline in popularity among executives and consultants. Such structures can certainly be helpful, but sometimes have worked to confuse and delay responsibilities and decision.

The activities of people in matrix organizations are directed by two or more lines of authority rather than a single chain of command. For instance, one hierarchical structure may be responsible for production while a second directs the professional disciplines or technologies required. Thus, there is a traditional line-manufacturing organization, and also an organization that manages the activities of mechanical or electronic engineers, for examples, who are also actively concerned with manufacturing the product.

At other, more senior levels in the company, still another management dimension may be added, such as geographic or product authority. At or near the manufacturing floor and direct sales levels, a matrix organization will usually introduce serious confusion, indecision, and conflict. Unless one authority line has clear and unmistakable pre-eminence in directing the actions of production supervisors and employees, for instance, there will be serious problems.

The first-level supervisor of a "clean room" manufacturing operation once told me that his most troublesome problem was deciding what to do when confronted with conflicting orders from his immediate manager to "ship product" and from the equally ranked and powerful engineering manager to "hold for further testing." Presumably, the motives of both managers were the same: to serve and satisfy the customer. From the young supervisor's description, resolution took one of three paths as follows:

1. Noisy confrontation between the managers resulting, finally, in a decision—often to ship some units and hold some for testing.
2. Decision by the supervisor himself when decision seemed unlikely. Usually, he said, he never heard about the matter again.
3. Referral to the manufacturing director (or even higher), who didn't understand why he had to make the decision when there were two perfectly competent managers involved who knew the issues better than he.

Professional employees, too, can be very uncomfortable if required to report to more than a single authority. A client of ours manufactured very sophisticated missile systems. Each system was virtually one of a kind because considerable engineering and design took place almost at the time each system was being constructed. In that situation, some managers were responsible for each of the primary component subsystems such as guidance, propulsion, and so forth. A second hierarchy of managers coordinated the actions of various technical discipline teams, such as electronics, mechanical, and flight test engineers. Meanwhile, of course, a third hierarchy was charged with actually building the things.

An individual engineer might, then, be accountable to both his or her functional leadership, such as electronic engineering, and also to a product or subsystem authority, such as the director of fail-safe manufacturing. Moreover, during the course of system manufacture, this same engineer might report to several subsystem executives as his or her professional skills and subsystem requirements dictated. For some, this was very uncomfortable, and they didn't like it.

For most, the dual authority lines, or the matrix, was satisfactory. This was a highly regarded company with very mature and experienced managers who had a long history of successful collaboration. And the focus of everyone was on the construction of a single, new system of great national importance. We found that the mature, collaborative style, the single product focus, and undoubted importance of the work combined to make this matrix organization effective. When such conditions do not exist, matrix organization forms often do not perform well because they introduce confusion and conflict about the basic purposes and meaning of the place. People can come to think that they are supposed to "do electrical engineering" instead of building missiles, in this example. Allegiances and loyalties can shift to a single profession, its leaders, and hierarchy and away from the mission of the enterprise.

Drawing reporting lines on paper, a hobby with many executives, is a long way from creating a more vital organization. Changing structure to support and reflect purpose is sound. But expect a period of reduced productivity while people sort out and try to accommodate to new roles, relationships, and, especially, expectations.

## SOME TYPICAL ORGANIZATION STRUCTURES

### Functional

Many companies use some variant of a column-shaped structure where specific business functions, such as accounting or human resources, report to progressively higher-level executives who represent the same function. A plant controller reports to a division-level controller who, in turn, reports to a corporate controller.

Some advantages include the following:

- Enhances functional independence and can provide alternate communication and reporting channels
- Attracts and trains functional specialists effectively
- Sets up balance of power among functions and fosters careful, deliberate decisions
- Diffuses power and tends to avoid major errors
- Promotes communication within specific functions

Some disadvantages include the following:

- Sets up turf and asset battles among functions
- Can be sluggish and slow to respond to changed circumstances
- Does not tend to produce generalists or general managers
- Can inhibit cross-function communication

## Product Line, Technology, Market, or Geographically Focused Structures

A company might be primarily organized around its specific products or product groups such as Hyundai's ship-building and automotive divisions or General Electric's appliance and power systems groups. Sometimes, technology is the primary organizing principle such as Hoechst-Celanese's fibers and chemicals divisions.

Companies with a comparatively narrow technology base, such as battery maker Duracell, may successfully organize some manufacturing, packaging, development, and distribution activities to concentrate on specific market segments, such as OEM customers, giant retailers, and small outlets.

The airlines offer basically one technology and one product, so they tend to be organized around geographic considerations such as their routes, or spokes, and hubs. Soft drink franchises are similarly structured.

### The Traditional Pyramid—Whether Tall or Flat

This is the most usual and familiar organization structure, typified by the military and the Church. Giant corporations such as the old (pre- 1983-1984) AT&T had this organization form. Today, the giant pyramid is often much flatter and smaller. Often, too, the once unified structure is now many, far smaller, pyramidal structures reporting to a comparatively small holding company or senior staff. American Home Products is a good example.

### Staff and Line Considerations

These once clearly separate types of functions are often merged today. The personnel or human resource function, for instance, was once viewed purely as a staff or support department. Today, there may be no personnel department at all. At Nucor Steel, most personnel responsibilities and activities are part of the plant general manager's role. In other companies, many staff functions have been contracted to outside firms. Payroll, benefit administration, employee assistance, and some aspects of employment and labor relations are frequently outsourced.

Large, especially global, corporations today may employ all of the organization forms briefly noted above. For instance, the structural units closest to the customers may be product line focused. These units may, in turn, be linked through a geographically defined structure that reports into a traditional corporate pyramid with functimnally aligned staff responsibilities. Meanwhile, there may be matrix structures elsewhere in the corporation.

Executives have a great many organization forms available. The task is to select or design a structure that communicates expectations and facilitates goal attainment through the firm's differentiation strategies.

### *SELF-MANAGED GROUPS (SMG)*

Since perhaps 1980, the tall organization pyramid has been shrinking. Whole management levels have been eliminated. Spans of control have expanded. In most successful firms, genuine decision authority and control have been pushed down, and out, to people who best know and understand the conditions within and near their environments, where goods and services are produced or where trade really occurs.

Sometimes such activities have been extensively publicized but with little real change made or intended. The most successful efforts have been both relatively quick and real. The results have sometimes been spectacular and almost always positive for trade. Firms as diverse as AT&T's manufacturing unit, now Lucent Technologies, and car maker Saturn have moved aggressively toward SMG's in just a few years.

A deliberate SMG strategy requires managerial courage, a long-term commitment, and a devotion to serious education. It demands experimentation and great tolerance for uncertainty at all organization levels, executive to production worker. Labor union leaders can feel out of control and threatened, just like managers. After all, if highly skilled groups handle traditional managerial duties such as schedules, coaching, discipline, and quality, group members clearly don't desire or require close supervision. Nor may they want or need union representation, at least not in the usual sense. This trend toward increasing authority nearer the task is, I believe, an irreversible, growing change of great significance.

There are three reasons that SMGs and other approaches to less direct supervision and enriched jobs generally succeed. They are as follows:

1. People closer to the problems are, or if trained, can be the most expert at solving many issues effectively.
2. Such strategies often directly and positively enhance quality, reduce cycle times, and cut costs, all components of a differentiation strategy.
3. SMGs can significantly increase member self-esteem through greater opportunities for achievement, recognition, control, and application of basic beliefs. This leads to great organization resilience and endurance.

Some observers have predicted that before long, a very large proportion of U.S. employees will work at home. Computer power, their argument runs, will permit such easy connectivity and information flow that there will be far less need for office environments. Home-based work is nothing new, of course. Artisans, physicians, farmers, and others worked from their homes long before the rise of giant corporations and offices. Many have never done otherwise.

I am not convinced that this trend toward the "virtual" corporation will be either as large or as individually satisfying as predicted. It is not necessary to accept the entire prediction to observe that, indeed, the computer revolution has permitted some major changes. The speed, accuracy, and accessibility of data have rendered many management and analyst-type positions less essential. In large measure, cheap, powerful, computer technology has permitted much of the job elimination and downsizing of the past decade. Economic demands drove downsizing; technology enabled it to occur.

As we learn to convert more data into decision-relevant information, leaders will continue to find more opportunities to flatten, decentralize, and downsize. When the task requires people to work closely together or where capital concentration is required in plants, offices, and factories, self-managed work groups are proving to be effective alternatives to the long, vertical chain of command. They can provide both great responsiveness to output requirements and also opportunities for the satisfaction of powerful human needs for self-respect and confidence.

# Chapter 7

# People

At the level of corporate strategy, leaders are charged with two parallel tasks:

1. Forging and constantly honing a sharp-edged, internally, cohesive clarity about the firm's purpose, character, and identity
2. Engaging internal creativity and energy to devise products and services that differentiate the firm in the eyes of its customers

As inhaling and exhaling are necessary for life, so are both identity and differentiation required for trade.

Identity, differentiation, and, ultimately, trade can only be achieved by committed people. No executive, no leader, can go very wrong who devotes a considerable portion of his or her time to seeing to it that every important position is filled with the most skilled, talented, and effective person available. There is no more important or appropriate use of executive power.

I am also persuaded that careful, sustained development of the competence and confidence of people is the most effective way to convert assets into real resources. In every case I have studied, the payback from such persistent investment has been enormous. But don't expect much from an occasional, off-the-shelf program. The development effort must be planned, sustained for years, and encompass all kinds of developmental experiences. An important extra benefit of such an approach is the continual refinement and renewed commitment to the firm's core identity and purpose.

Each employee needs to understand and personally accept as valid and proper the purposes of the organization and how its goals will be achieved—the organization's differentiation methods. This will help to assure the dedication of carefully selected and talented people to the goals of the enterprise. No one who is personally offended by the primary purposes, actions, and methods of an organization can serve it well. The reverse is also true. People who believe in and identify with the firm's intentions and purposes are likely to succeed. If the basic personality and identity of the company conflicts with your values and beliefs, seek another employer. The price of staying on is likely to be a painful loss of self-respect and poor performance. Our firm has rejected some potential clients for that reason. Leaders are, or should be, accountable for defining, explaining, and translating the meaning of the company. It is an endless task, and a critical one.

An understanding and acceptance of the purposes of the organization is important. In addition, each of us wants to be both clear and reasonably comfortable about what others expect of us, and what we may expect from others. This seems almost self-evident, but a great many people simply do not know what is expected of them at work, a condition that breeds unnecessary tentativeness and insecurity. "Knowing what is expected" does not necessarily mean a mechanistic or restrictive job description. Rather, it is a sense of one's place and fit—one's primary relationships, measures, support, and responsibilities. True leaders at any level do their best to personally communicate expectations over and over again and to devise many techniques for reaching more remote members.

Finally, leaders are responsible for seeing to it that conditions of work provide clear opportunities for enhanced personal confidence through achievement, recognition, personal influence, and reinforcement of basic beliefs. Only leaders can define what achievement is and how it will be recognized in a particular enterprise. Corporate-level staff positions, even high-level ones, often provide little opportunity for personal growth or for enhanced self-confidence through achievement, simply because no expectations of consequence accompany the job.

Recently, an outstanding manufacturing executive we know was promoted into a newly created, high-level corporate staff role. He's now in charge of "corporate diversity" for a widely scattered, $8 billion (sales) company. It is likely a rotational assignment, but he is still uneasy.

I have no idea what the definitions are, let alone the goals. Other than the obvious, there aren't any measures or standards that I can see. No authority comes with this job, so any plant or division manager can tell me to buzz off, and I expect they will. Hell, they've got products and customers to worry about. I've about decided to study this diversity thing to death, maybe call a meeting or two, and go visit some other companies. I won't accomplish anything useful, but my corporate ticket will be punched so I can get back to manufacturing.

Only leaders can structure the organization and change processes to allow people greater opportunities to exert power, control, and influence. Insecure leaders are rarely willing to do so. When he took over as chairman and CEO of the Brunswick Corporation, Jack Reichert set about devolving power from corporate to the divisions. He cut corporate staff by about 80 percent and eliminated all sorts of corporate-level approvals of divisional actions. Gradually, the division executives began to act like the CEOs of mostly autonomous businesses. Jack wanted to push most authority still further down—to the operating plants. In this he was only partly successful. Some division heads lacked the essential self-confidence to release any of their power—to take the risk that someone down the line might make a mistake.

It is hard to overstate the importance of these conditions to individual energy, commitment, and creative dedication. Even now, after decades of work with owners, executives, and professionals in a host of different settings, I am sometimes surprised by how few are clear about the importance of the following three factors:

- organization purpose,
- clear personal expectations, and
- individual self-confidence.

Organizations of all kinds are changing dramatically. My neighbor is a highly trained doctor in a large clinic. He is experiencing radical, disconcerting change in all three areas.

I used to think my purpose and the clinic's purpose were the same . . . to help sick people. Now the owners, all doctors, and the administrators are concerned mostly with making money and even the survival of the clinic. It has totally changed how we all relate to one another, and not for the better. We've cut back the nursing staff and there's pressure to see more patients. There's even subtle pressure to refer patients internally rather than to an outsider. I don't know what the place is becoming, but I know I don't like it, and I don't like me for putting up with it. That's not what the practice of medicine should be.

A lot of company executives and managers well understand such intense feelings as these. They inevitably accompany a loss of self-respect.

It is not nearly enough to simply send personnel requisitions over to the human resource department. Organization leaders must provide that department with the clear expectations and the resources necessary to attract, select, employ, and retain top-level talent suited to the specific position and for the future. That requirement means a continuing, effective recruiting effort, validated selection methods, thorough background verifications, fully competitive compensation levels, effective training, and many other conditions. Perhaps the most vital condition for effective staffing is to establish clear and honest expectations, even if uncertain in key respects. Honesty and, where possible, clear expectations are especially important during any major transition. That is when the psychological and physical loss of productive people is most damaging and most likely. In my experience, most people readily understand and can accept an executive's forthright statement of uncertainty and inability to change outside market or economic conditions. They are also quick to spot false assurances. Executives who repeatedly overpromise to investment analysts, for instance, are likely to earn the contempt of many employees.

Just recently the general manager of a 3,000-employee manufacturing operation fulminated to me about his company's CEO:

What the hell is he doing? This is the third time he's promised the analysts a 15 percent increase and it will be the third time we miss it by a lot. Why does he lie to them? We can't do it and everyone knows it. He's out of touch completely.

Once the investment has been made to employ the talented people required for long-term achievement, it is folly to squander such assets. Yet that is just what often happens when organization leaders permit conditions to exist that reduce or destroy self-confidence and commitment, or when top leaders fail to be explicit with each executive about what is expected and how he or she will be measured.

In conditions of radical organization change, it is especially vital to reexamine the implied, informal, or assumed contract between the organization and its employees. Not long ago, the implied contract described, essentially, a continuous trade between employer and employee. If the employee performed his or her duties well, demonstrated loyalty, and created minimal discomfort in others, employment until retirement was virtually guaranteed. Salaried, professionally skilled people could rely on this implied contract with nearly the same assurance that union members could depend on their written contract.

Beginning, perhaps, in the early 1970s both implied and formal employment contracts began to fray at the edges. As many companies began to struggle to redefine their trade purposes, the expectations between people and firms started to shift. Only ten years later, even more change was evident in bellwether organizations such as AT&T and GM. Perhaps a decade after that, the implied, or written, safety net of mutual expectations had largely disintegrated. No one is safe, not professional or manager, executive or union member.

A few years ago, detailed employment contracts were not uncommon even for midlevel management and professional people. Today they seem to be increasingly rare for any but top-level leaders. I've seen several recent employment agreements that must be signed before hiring. They state that ". . . either the firm or the individual may end the employment relationship at any time, with or without notice and for any reason, or no reason." The agreements go on to state that there is no expressed or implied period of employment involved in the relationship.

Sometimes people considerations can become the driver of remarkable organization renewal. A joint-venture partner of our firm was originally a team of about twenty engineers, chemists, physicists, and designers, who had years before formed a company to design hardware under subcontract to a major defense manufacturer. The reduction in defense spending and the end of a particular contract spelled near-term collapse. The firm's members, together, decided that real strength lay in their diverse yet complementary skills and collegial style of working well together. As a team, they determined to become a broad-gauged product development specialist for any industry or firm, not just defense industries. Today, there are about 150 people engaged in the development of new toys, home electronics, and medical instruments, among others. Changes in their way of differentiating themselves, through organization structure and internal systems, all followed a thorough evaluation of staff abilities and commitment. It resulted in a decision to ultimately rely on staff competence, interpersonal confidence, and cohesion to achieve success.

I believe changes in mutual expectations between firms and people will have profound influence for the next several decades at least. When the social, psychological, and economic history is written, this fracturing of the implied contract will be shown to have been often necessary, sometimes brutal, and frequently pivotal to regaining the ability to trade successfully. For the hundreds of thousands of discharged professional and managerial people, the financial and psychological consequences have been enormous. Listen carefully and you can already hear echoes of 1930s era cautions, concerns, and worries. A lot of sons and daughters will grow up hearing about the instability, anguish, and downsizings of the past twenty years.

Tightly controlled or bureaucratic organizations tend to restrict member opportunities to gain self-confidence. By their nature, controlling organizations allow and reward a more limited range of alternative behaviors than those that are smaller or more entrepreneurial. Long-term people who are suddenly dismissed from strongly controlling firms seem to have a more difficult time than those who leave less restrictive environments. The threatened financial situations may be very similar, yet those dismissed from less controlling, less structured environments seem to recover much more rapidly. I know of managers dismissed from large, household name companies several years ago who have yet to regain a positive sense of self-worth and value. They remain underemployed, essentially sad, fearful, and depressed. Too proud to apply for unemployment compensation, more than a few have simply given up, apparently unable to behave in ways essential to rebuilding careers and lost self-respect. Perhaps their long, successful histories in a controlling environment eventually restricted their behavioral repetoires, and flexibility. The very attributes that led to success in a controlled, predictable world seem to be major handicaps in conditions of fluid uncertainty.

It is not reasonable to expect most people who matured in relatively structured, controlling environments to suddenly become solo entrepreneurs, though that is exactly what some have advocated. Only a few can, and fewer will. Most people displaced from structured environments are better advised to find and select a work situation that offers a familiar level of procedure and clarity of expectation, even if the new environment is smaller and pays less. These often very talented people, if realistic in their expectations, can offer smaller employers valuable skills and experiences. In so doing, many will become reenergized and refocused on helping their new company to trade successfully and thereby rebuild their personal self-confidence.

## BURNOUT

Much has been written about the apparently increasing frequency of burnout. In my experience burnout is most likely to be discussed, and its symptoms observed, among staff or support people, especially those with managerial titles, whose work is relatively distant from the firm's customers and from the production and sale of its products or services. Unlike many of their peers in operating units, corporate and support people and many midlevel managers find it difficult to experience genuine, measurable achievement or to exercise much visible influence, two vital contributors to self-esteem. I suspect, too, that burnout results from steadily, and sometimes radically, increased expectations imposed both by the individual and by more senior executives as a consequence of staff reductions and demands for ever-higher levels of financial performance.

In many companies, the number of supporting staff and midlevel managers has been dramatically reduced. But executive expectations, tasks, and requirements have not. The same reports, studies, analyses, and activities are demanded as before, when the staff was much larger. Leaders, managers, and support people need to mutually reexamine and renegotiate roles and expectations. Many "nice-to-have" systems, documents, and processes can and should be scaled down or eliminated altogether to fit the reduced availability of people.

But it is not only leader expectations that drive the sometimes frantic level of activity and feelings of anxious exhaustion we call burnout. Incumbents in many management and professional positions continue to accept and even to create entirely new responsibilities to be added to their already overburdened roles, perhaps in an effort to become indispensable or to hide from frustration and feelings of insecurity. Whatever the reason, the level of unfocused, frenetic activity we increasingly see in client offices is often dysfunctional to the company and harmful to the individuals concerned. Very little of it adds anything to the organization's ability to trade successfully. Executive leaders need to find out how lower positioned people feel and then to respond appropriately. "Feel good," stress-reduction-type workshops are not the answer—realistic assignments and fewer priorities are, together with openly communicated expectations.

As the historic expectations between employer and employee have changed, new working relationships have begun to evolve. Some have been made possible, though not caused, by advances in technology. Similar technologies have permitted and even accelerated dramatic reductions in the ranks of middle-level managers and others. But technology is not causing the continuing reductions—the trade imperative is. Paradoxically, some of the conditions that have impelled leaders into massive, continuous downsizings are likely to be made even more debilitating by the resulting loss of company coherence, and employee self-confidence.

## OUTSOURCING

Among the evolving staffing methodologies is a striking increase in subcontracting and outsourcing. Leaders in firms of all kinds and sizes are reexamining their differentiation postures and determining to concentrate the energies of their own people on activities that more visibly and directly support the purposes of the company. Other necessary, but not directly trade-supporting, functions are being contracted to outside firms. Automatic Data Processing Corporation, ADP, has prospered for decades by handling the entire payroll function for many companies. Payroll is a specialized and critical function that must be done right and on time. In most firms the payroll function does not visibly support product or service differentiation, so hundreds of large and small companies contract with ADP and its competitors to handle payroll. Not companies alone, but also cities and counties, are contracting with others to perform specific services. Many elected officials have found the courage to direct public-sector or government managers to contract for trash collection, facilities management, and other functions. These officials are examining the purpose of city government, the equivalent of redefining the government's tax for service posture. In many public and private organizations, a new set of management skills will be required: selecting and managing contingent employees and firms.

Leaders are regularly contracting to others activities that were once viewed as inviolate. For instance, we work with several client executives who have virtually eliminated their product development departments. They have contracted with outside specialists to develop new products, from concept through prototype. Others have eliminated inside tax, personnel, audit, public relations, and systems groups. Selected parts of these traditional activities have been assigned to outside specialists because they were not judged to be central to the primary purposes of the company. There is no apparent limit to the growth of outsourcing: Hospitals now contract with groups of physicians to handle their emergency rooms; dental surgeons have specialist groups on retainer to handle more complex anesthesias. The list goes on. To the extent that outsourcing enhances strategic cohesion, it is likely to prove beneficial over the longer term. It can serve to condense, coalesce, and sharpen the character of the firm and enhance its identity in the eyes of its customers.

## *TEMPORARY EMPLOYMENT*

As with outsourcing, there have always been temporary employees. Also, similar to outsourcing, there has been a large increase in both the number of such employees and in the variety of skills temporarily engaged. Today, senior executives, research chemists, lawyers, and doctors are temporary employees. Virtually every profession and skill is readily available for hire on a temporary basis.

No longer is temporary employment limited to individuals. Entire industrial sales forces and factory manufacturing groups are engaged by firms on an as-needed basis. This has long been true in financial auditing, farming, and retail sales, for example. In recent years, temporary employment of entire functional groups has greatly expanded. Particularly in cyclical, changing, or seasonal businesses, it is an obvious way to add temporary muscle without adding permanent cost and distraction.

Just as important, though rarely acknowledged, ending a temporary employment relationship with an individual or group is far less traumatic than firing or laying off permanent people. It is easier for managers and employees. No one's expectations are suddenly violated, no one's self-esteem is destroyed, nor is the firm's cohesion fractured, as so often happens when long-term employees are forced out. The contracted time is over, the task is complete, and the deliverables have been presented; we can part without feelings of guilt or anger.

Because the employer-employee contract is, today, so fragile and individual self-image less and less linked to service with a particular organization, many highly trained professionals prefer to sell their services on a short-term basis. The desires of such individuals and the strategies of many organizations are mutually supporting.

## BUSINESS PROCESS REENGINEERING (BPE)

BPE, under different names, has been around for a very long time. More recently it has become the primary product of some giant consulting and business advisory firms. As it is typically sold, BPE is a programmatic, often linear way to evaluate and reconceptualize the basic internal processes of an organization. In theory, every important internal activity and system is scrutinized to see whether and how much value it adds for the cost incurred. BPE is a top-down procedure that, conceptually at least, has much in common with time and motion measurement and short-interval scheduling techniques.

In practice, many senior executives who have had firsthand experience with BPE initiatives are dissatisfied with the result. They describe BPE projects as too much, too fast and as superficial. Managers say that often the real purpose, as they later came to understand, is to provide a cover, a rational, for simply reducing staff. They say that the real objective quickly becomes apparent to employees at all levels. The all too frequent result is a demoralized workforce and considerable real, but disguised, opposition that often vitiates any lasting savings. BPE is typically bought, and sold, as a systems improvement effort. In practice, it is often experienced as a somewhat dishonest cover for staff reductions.

Refocusing initiatives coupled with acquisition driven staff reductions, layoffs, and removals of entire organization levels have largely invalidated the implied contract between employer and employed. I think we can foresee some significant consequences.

Many managers and professionals in aerospace industries have long "followed the contracts." If their employer lost a contract, many abruptly left to sign on with an expanding firm. Their loyalty and commitment was to themselves and their profession, not to any particular employer. Much the same was true of systems analysts and computer programmers in the 1970s and early 1980s. The market for such people was robust, and many took full advantage. They followed advancement opportunities, salary growth, and technology. In the future, I expect that we will see much increased movement from company to company by skilled people of all kinds, not solely by highly paid professionals. Many more will become floating, full-time, temporary employees while others establish their own entrepreneurial businesses.

This trend will be accelerated by a near-certain continuation of corporate contraction in some industries. It will be enhanced by an aging population, the trend toward low population growth, and by the failure of schools and colleges to graduate the required number of people able to contribute in many fields.

Working against this trend, it should be noted, is less willingness to move geographically by an ever older work force. Increased immigration will also limit the impact somewhat. But if the economy is reasonably strong, I think it inevitable that more of those who can do so will reduce their commitment to any single employer. The implied contract will continue to erode in many industries and locations, though not all. There are, of course, companies and facilities in more attractive or remote areas that will largely escape the trend. Still, on balance, the informal contract is becoming undependable for most employers and most employees.

My son is a young, highly trained engineer. When I ask his friends, none say they expect to stay with any company more than a few years. They are loyal to themselves and to a vision of what they think their professional lives should be. Their self-concept and confidence is entirely separate from association with any employer.

> Look, the top brass don't care about the division or us. They'd sell out in a minute. So what's the profit in being loyal?

## THE CONTRACT

This change in the dependability of the implied contract is a tectonic-plate level movement, slow and probably irreversible. It is already beginning to change the structure and strategies of personnel and human resource departments and of the services and benefits they manage. One large, high technology client has scaled back from about 160,000 employees to about 50,000, and there will be still more staff reductions. Top executives and others have noticed that the firm's professional and managerial people now rarely stay after 5:00 p.m. Very few come to work on weekends or holidays. Less than a decade ago, it was normal to see people and teams in on weekends and at all hours. The commitment and energy were evident. For these people, the implied contract and expectations were clear and alive. The company offered top-level benefits, security, marvelous career opportunities, and high pay in return. Assets were willingly advanced for promising developments. Then came the massive employment contractions, and everything changed. You could argue, as some executives do, that the new work behaviors and expectations are more balanced and actually more healthy for employees and their families. Perhaps so. But survivors tell me that it isn't nearly so alive, exciting, or challenging as it once was. As one survivor says:

We've lost what we had and what we were. Today we're no different and no better than a bunch of others. There's nothing that sets us apart like there once was.

This statement describes a firm without coherent identity or much differentiation in the eyes of its employees. The company's financial reports say that many customers feel the same way. Maybe recurring downsizings have been necessary for survival, but in many cases, one has to ask just what has really survived.

So, what should the new "contract" be? What should pay, hours, and benefits be for employees whose self-concept and self-confidence are increasingly less dependent on their employer or conditions of work? And who are manifestly less willing to invest in that activity? It is by no means clear.

## SELECTION

We know a great deal about how to select people who will likely perform well in many occupations. There is an enormous, research-based literature on the subject that spans more than a half century. Few employers, though, use more than a very primitive recruitment and selection process. A few court rulings and much overcautious legal advice have apparently frightened a lot of leaders away from using demonstrably fair and effective employee selection methods, that can inexpensively and substantially improve the likelihood that a particular person will succeed. If a firm's identity and intentions call for fewer but more highly competent people who will contribute ever more to the success of its trade and differentiation strategies, one suggestion is to greatly improve the vetting of employees at all levels.

Similarly, with increasing use of outsourcing and temporary employees, fully qualifying prospective outside firms and individuals is vital. I can tell you with assurance that within our consulting specialty, not one assignment in four is awarded to us based on a careful verification of the competing firms' references, reputations, and competencies. Likewise, temporary employees often appear at the door with nothing more than the temporary help agency's assurance that the people sent are fully qualified. The references and backgrounds of prospective full-time, senior-level employees are also only occasionally verified. During the past quarter century, a fair number of our firm's top people have been lured away or have otherwise left for new opportunities. In only one case—one—has a prospective employer sought to verify the departing employee's position, responsibilities, or performance. Senior executive friends and clients report similar experiences. I have long been bemused by leaders who engage new people for important, even critical, posts with less care than they would use in buying a car.

One day soon a new leadership skill or discipline will emerge that encompasses finding, vetting, contracting, and managing external resource individuals and groups. Companies that perform these functions really well will have a major advantage over their competitors.

As vital as selecting suitable people is now, it will become a leadership responsibility of even greater importance in the future. And as critical as people selection is, it is no more so than establishing the kinds of conditions at work that enable talented, carefully selected people to contribute and flourish as you hoped they would in the first place. People, for all their complexity and perversity, are the primary drivers of change.

# Chapter 8

# Systems

Along with people, organization, and assets, leaders also have a large measure of control over the organization's formal systems that inform, communicate, report, and control. Systems can be primary levers of change. Without dependable systems, no leader can know how the firm and each operating unit is performing. Systems permit the reliable assessment of strategic accomplishment and of the performance of assets, units, and individuals.

In my view, a system is any methodology intended to measure, analyze, and, especially, communicate the present status and defined changes in any variable, any selected factor that can meaningfully change. In military terminology, important systems should meet one or more of four primary functions. Large systems serve all four of the following:

- Command
- Control
- Communication
- Intelligence

Not surprisingly, the functions of massive DOD systems are often abbreviated and described as $C^3I$ systems. Relatively few seem to work as intended and all have been enormously expensive. Even so, it isn't a bad description of what systems are supposed to do.

Viewed this way, a system can be an elaborate, multifaceted, and even multinational computer-driven report package. Or it can be some numbers and notes handwritten on the back of an envelope. By definition and in practice, a system does not require anything to be written, printed, or permanently recorded. In fact, the most effective systems in most companies are informal communications from one person or one group to another. Important as they are, I have never seen a strategically important decision taken solely or even largely on the basis of the output of any single, formal system. Perhaps the closest to system determination of behavior are the actions of an airline pilot in response to information provided by many systems. But interpretation and judgment are always paramount in the cockpit. Every captain ultimately relies on his training, experience, and judgement. Systems do not decide very many important matters; people do. Fuzzy set theory, for instance, has promise as a way of making formal systems more nearly reflect human decision-making processes, the way you and I tend to think. But for now, most systems can directly control only fairly trivial events. They can and do provide much information through the intelligence function in the $C^3I$ abbreviation. Utility and cost are the only proper measures of a system, not its specific content or complexity.

Companies, small or large, are complicated. Nearly anything about them can change, and often does. Some changes are important, most are not. The challenge lies in deciding what factors count and what changes are truly important. Every month, one heavy-equipment manufacturing company we work with issues a three- to four-inch thick report to every department head in every facility, worldwide. The cost is considerable. Department managers who receive the report agree unanimously that only two pages of the document and four or five measures have any value to them. Moreover, because the report shows only long past information, it spurs little action.

As one manager suggested:

> Give us only the five measures we really need. Get those to us, at least every week or, better, every day. Don't worry about the last two decimal places. Then we can make things happen.

This manager makes the following important points:

- Track only a few carefully chosen and designed measurements; those that show deviation from the path or from important objectives that will help add to future trade in some way. Everything else is history.

- Invite those who need the information to decide what it should be, to what level of precision, and how often.
- Provide the required measures only to the level of accuracy that is useful to those who will use the information.
- Provide the information fast and often to those who can act.

The purpose of any system, any report, any document, or any measurement should be to advance one or more key differentiation strategies. Any that don't meet that standard or are not required for legal reasons should be dropped. My rough estimate is that less than half of existing business systems do either. Just as with the other architectural elements, leaders often have less than complete control over an organization's systems. Certainly, leaders can cause the design, selection, and purchase of computers and software. They can direct the intensive training of employees who will use the systems. Even so, the company's norms, history, beliefs, and relationships will see to it that much additional information of undetermined accuracy will be informally gathered and communicated. The less that formal systems meet people's real information needs, the more that various, informal systems will take over. A firm's systems include far more than information gathering, analysis, and dissemination; there is always an attached network of policies, procedures, and accepted "ways we do things around here."

A client of ours requires very large quantities of a particular kind of fabric. The purchasing department dutifully selects vendors, orders, and procures the fabric at the best price available. The system works well. The problem is that once the material is logged into the storerooms, nearly anyone can enter, cut off, and remove whatever quantity is desired for repairs, experiments, or prototypes. As a result, stock outs and production delays are common. Extra costs to quickly obtain needed material, higher work in process levels, and missed customer shipments are among the extra expenses incurred. The firm's reporting systems accurately reflect purchases, but completely unrelated systems report raw material inventories, work in process, and other key measurements up to a month later. Only now are managers beginning to resolve this systems-based problem. In a time of great hardware and software sophistication, such a situation as this may seem unusual. It is not, I assure you.

The way managers and other employees have coped with this long-term problem is to take every opportunity to build hidden stockpiles of the fabric, here and there, for use when the stockrooms run out. An informal system has evolved that usually keeps the plant operating and customers supplied, despite an inadequate formal system. At one level, the informal system is useful, even essential. But consider what these practices do to the accuracy of important financial reports and product-costing decisions, to name just two.

In another common instance, an inventory reporting system shows an analyst that there aren't enough screws of a certain kind in the stockroom to fill projected production needs. Instead of simply ordering the screws, the analyst must obtain two higher level approval signatures, take the approved order to a specified purchasing agent, and so on. The system accurately shows that expeditious action is needed. But all the associated practices add time, and therefore costs, to what should be a simple transaction. They also add to the risk of being out of stock and could delay shipment to an unhappy customer.

Abarta, Inc., is a substantial, privately held, soft drink, energy, and publishing enterprise. Like many companies, the end of every month was a frantic time because month-end inventory, sales, and other results were reported. Achieving the aggressively demanded month-end numbers had become the driving motivation for many disruptive, and expensive, short-term expedients that added no value to the firm or to its customers. John Bitzer, Abarta's CEO, knew that adding to company value and customer satisfaction requires a longer-term perspective. He instituted new systems that let every general manager know his or her results every day, but reported period averages to corporate only every quarter. John and his general managers are delighted with the healthy changes in decision-making behavior that have flowed from the systems redesign. Now the individual business-unit managers concentrate on matters that drive long-term success, not on meeting some imposed, short-term numbers.

Any system, together with its associated practices and other appendages, should visibly support one or more differentiation purposes or legal requirements. If it does not, if it only increases the sense of managerial security and control, it is a prime candidate for dismantling or redesign. Often, leaders can and should become personally involved in determining the purposes and specific outputs of important systems. Without such clarity from the leaders, their requests, questions, and preferences may inadvertently lead others to put in place systems that cause entirely unexpected and even unwanted actions. Many companies have expensive reporting systems in place that were created originally to provide one-time answers to a leader's question.

Systems, and all that goes with them, sometimes seem to be immortal. Organization leaders must demonstrate vigorous leadership and take an active, often personal role in the systems area. It is one of the four architectural factors that cannot be wholly delegated and where executive focus can have great impact. Whatever variables are measured, reported, and, especially, paid for are exactly those that will attract, focus, and absorb subordinates' time and energy. Design every system and every measure to focus only on what is truly important for strategic advantage, and that is where energy and attention will be directed. Measure marginally important changes, and you will squander great time and energy.

Years ago I was a member of a research team that studied the human factors involved in high-reliability manufacturing. The research was performed for several governmental agencies that funded the work equally. Every week each of us was required to list the hours and separate tasks performed for each agency. Since the entire project was unitary, it was not possible to accurately make such distinctions. Even so, every week we devoted hours to developing necessarily fictional time and task allocations.

All of us need to know what we are expected to concentrate upon and accomplish, and we need to know what is important to our leaders and our organization. Without clear, credible, and frequent information about what is important, we will fasten on other signs and signals to point the way. What is measured and reported is paramount among the signs and signals people use to define what is important and what is expected. Be careful what you ask for.

Just because technology permits easy dissemination of nearly limitless data does not mean that it necessarily should. There are companies that produce copies of awesomely detailed reports for each of their 25,000 employees. The intent is good, but not always well-considered. For instance, production floor employees and supervisors regularly get detailed numbers about sales costs and facility property taxes, neither of which they can directly influence. Should employees have such information? Perhaps. But how often and to what level of detail? Direct and design systems to provide regular information to those who have substantial influence and in a form they can use to diagnose and solve real problems.

Even with highly sophisticated $C^3I$ systems in place, most information in most firms will pass informally from person to person. Humans are social animals. The workplace can serve as a vehicle to meet many psychological needs, the most important of which is self-respect. Such needs can be partly met through frequent, semi-structured opportunities for communication across functional and geographic lines and organization levels. Encourage the informal information system to work. It will always be far ahead of and usually more believed than elaborate, after-the-fact formal systems.

One especially vital system that is largely under management control is compensation. Many organizations, probably most, continue to use a very structured, easily administered grade-level approach. In such plans each position is slotted into a grade level which, in turn, has a possible pay range. Raise percentages are pre-determined by management or by bargaining, in the case of union members. As a practical matter, most people in a particular grade level typically get about the same base pay and raises. In theory, differences in evaluated performance are supposed to be reflected in higher or lower raise amounts. They often are, but the actual differences are small. Compensation systems like these provide essentially no financial incentive, recognition, or reward for outstanding results. The real purposes of such systems are simple and mechanistic administrative stability and the appearance of fairness regardless of real performance. These systems often pay for the judged size or complexity of the *position,* not the skills and effectiveness of the person temporarily occupying the job. With many fewer management people and hierarchy levels, there are far more frequent changes in position requirements and also movement among positions today than only a decade ago. Positions come and go; success depends on performing people. Pay for skills and outcomes, not for titles and position size, as most compensation systems do.

Bill Neal, chairman of software provider Broadway and Seymour, Inc., was dissatisfied with the job-grade type of compensation system.he inherited. It paid all branch executives about the same, based on a simplistic evaluation of the position. The problem was that the branches were largely autonomous business units, operating in very different markets with very different products. Some branches had a long established customer base and mature products. Others were in a start-up mode with few customers, brand new products, and new people.

Working closely with Bill and the branch executives, we devised a unique compensation system based on a business and product, life cycle approach. Some branches would be expected to generate large profits while others were more properly measured on acquiring top-quality people, obtaining new customers, or successful new product introductions. Each branch was "spotted" along the life cycle curve and a compensation system was devised to encourage and reward outcomes appropriate to the status of the branch.

More and more leading firms are moving toward genuine incentive and pay-for-performance systems. Even in union environments, various "gainsharing" approaches are in frequent use. These typically share productivity gains, above some set level, between the company and its employees after removing the contribution of company paid capital improvements.

In companies with self-managed work groups, pay incentives are sometimes earned by separate teams whose members decide how to divide the "pot." Salaried people, including managers and professionals, are frequently eligible for very substantial incentive checks depending on measured company, unit, and personal performance. PepCom Industries' president, Allen Fleischer, implemented a system whereby first-level supervisors and others can apply for a quickly awarded spot bonus on behalf of any employee who demonstrates valued behaviors or specific achievements. That seems simple enough, but it took supervisors and managers several years to learn how to use the system to shape employee behaviors.

Effective, measured incentive pay systems must meet a few standards.

1. The objectives or standards used must be transparent and felt to be fair, so must the progress measurements employed.
2. Potential incentives need to be large enough to be truly meaningful to individual employees.
3. The standards against which achievements are to be measured must be carefully set. Too high and the motivation value will be lost, too low or too easy and the cost will become excessive for the gain.
4. Generally, it is best for incentive payments to be available quickly after the desired achievement.

The evidence seems clear that well-conceived, conscientiously administered incentive systems do drive economic gain—they support increased trade. The typical, grade-based pay systems have little impact on measured achievement, either individual or corporate. To return to an earlier example, Nucor Steel's compensation system pays a base rate significantly below the industry average. But output-based incentive pay can be and often is very substantial. Nucor employees frequently earn far more than their peers in other companies. The same basic compensation approach is used for millworkers and executives. The pay system molds and rewards behaviors and decisions that support successful trade. It has also proven to be a magnet for attracting talented, achievement-driven people. On a cost-per-ton basis, Nucor leads both its United States and Japanese competitors.

The CEO of a client manufacturing firm (industrial fasteners, blades, etc.) had about decided to reluctantly close a less profitable plant. For about a decade, surveys and other indicators had shown a higher than average level of employee confidence, loyalty, and commitment. We successfully persuaded the CEO to delay closing the plant. Instead, dozens of performance graphs were posted everywhere that showed actual against required plant performance. Copies were mailed to every employee's home that showed such indicators as:

- Cost per unit produced
- Defects per unit
- Production time (per unit)

- Scrap produced per unit built
- Customer satisfaction levels and comments

The CEO invested in substantial retraining, some new equipment, and dozens of work and paper-flow process changes. Two marginally effective plant executives were dismissed; one was replaced. Self-managed groups and operator verification of quality were introduced, as was an incentive-based pay system that applied to *every* employee.

Once they knew what was needed and how to get there, this committed group of employees reached—and then surpassed—the new standards. Today the once failing plant is the most efficient in the company.

The days when most people expect to occupy a single position in a particular company for many years are passing or gone in many firms. Tasks and specific jobs are increasingly short-lived. People move into and out of such temporary positions much more frequently than just a few years ago. Pay systems should reflect this condition by offering compensation based on individual skills, competencies, and achievements, not the presumed title or size of a position that, in any event, is likely to change or disappear altogether.

Some additional, people-oriented systems can also greatly influence a firm's ability to compete successfully. We have already considered compensation and employment systems; but there are others, such as:

- Management succession and early talent identification
- Validated performance appraisals that really motivate
- Diagnostic employee surveys of attitudes and opinions
- Customer surveys about satisfaction with products, services, and transactions

Large companies should have most of these kinds of systems in place and proven, while smaller firms may need only one or two. The question is not whether a particular organization has one or more systems with names like those above. The issue is whether the intent of each system is met and, most important, whether it advances company purpose, progress, and cohesion.

Leaders cannot successfully leave the determination of important systems and system outputs to functional specialists. The risks and the opportunities are too great.

## CULTURE

Much has been written about corporate culture, that cluster, or system, of history, beliefs, norms, values, and style that describes ". . . what we are and how we do things around here." Culture is an undeniably powerful determiner of how people tend to act in organizations. Especially in large, old, and relatively stable organizations, culture can be a primary guide to understanding the firm. Culture is much harder to describe and a less reliable compass in new or rapidly changing organizations.

Culture is often a powerful factor, but it is rarely an element that is realistically available to executives for achieving the firm's primary purpose—trade. Only rarely is culture a primary lever, equal in importance to assets, organization, people, or systems.

Sometimes, culture can be such a lever, but only over an extended time, and only as a consequence of a crisp, long-term focus on the four architectural elements. Culture is a real system but often very amorphous. It is hard to touch, feel, define, and measure. And it is nearly impossible to deliberately change a corporation's culture rapidly, significantly, or directly. The reality is, that without almost cataclysmic events, a company's culture will change only very slowly, like the slow movement of the earth's crust. Long before the culture changes, there will have been many alterations in the four architectural elements and in the strategic coherence of the firm.

For instance, many aspects of the cultures of the old AT&T, IBM, and DEC (Digital Equipment Corporation) have changed. Many aspects, but far from all. In all three situations, there were earthquakes in the environment both internal and external to the company. In all three, the cultures are still changing and evolving to cope with a new reality. All four architectural features have been and continue to be changed, though not always clearly or dramatically. Even in smaller companies, culture change takes years. In the five years since he became CEO of PepCom, Allen Fleischer has worked all four architectural elements to dramatically change the fear-dominated, repressive culture he inherited. There's a lot of financial and other evidence that he is succeeding, but another two or three years will probably be needed.

Culture is like happiness, a consequence of many things. Neither happiness nor culture can be readily grasped, pursued, defined, or measured. But both are important.

## *STYLE*

In my view, style is primarily an individual, personal characteristic. It is of greatest importance in face-to-face kinds of relationships and as a shaper and molder of leader-driven systems. But style is not easy to capture. To some, style can mean establishing clear expectations and providing firm procedures, and to others, it means demonstrating a concern for the wants and needs of people. To some, style describes the decisions that can be made and by whom. Yet another view defines style in terms of the amount, frequency, and veracity of information provided.

With enough time and focus, the prevailing style of most organizations can be altered toward greater employee inclusion, influence, and involvement, for instance. In larger organizations, it requires years for a significant change in executive-level style to be perceived, let alone widely emulated at lower levels in the hierarchy. More than one CEO has been frustrated to see that his vigorous efforts to alter company style faded away one or two levels down the chain of command.

Where individual style can make a major, usually rapid difference is in the quality and effectiveness of person-to-person relationships, especially between a superior and a subordinate. A change in the person or behavior of a small-plant manager, department head, group leader, or line supervisor can dramatically impact unit performance and morale. This, alone, is a sound and sufficient reason to devote significant effort and assets to the selection, compensation, and training of small-unit and lower-level leaders. Our own employee survey data clearly show that the most important single determiner of production, professional, or office worker commitment and morale is the quality of the relationship with one's immediate supervisor. This is equally true in union and non-union environments and appears to be independent of the kind or location of the business.

Style is a critically important and relatively fast-acting variable in the effective leadership of smaller, cohesive groups and sub-units. It is very much less so in large, dispersed, multilevel organizations. It is just not a directly accessible, management change lever in larger contexts, except as it influences the characteristics of important systems.

## *SUMMARY*

Trade is the only reason for companies to exist. Those that do so successfully will survive and prosper. All of the other desirable things that may be achieved are consequences, not primary company purposes or measures of leader success.

Causing successful trade is, therefore, every senior leader's prime task and is how his or her effectiveness should properly be judged. To achieve it, leaders have available four powerful levers of change. All four have the advantages of controllability, visibility, and, often, rapid effect. They shape the core identity of the firm and define how it will differentiate itself-in the market.

How successfully and how rapidly adjusting the levers will bring about meaningful change is always heavily influenced and often determined by the commitment and self-confidence of people—the firm's employees.

# SECTION III:
# THE MANAGEMENT OF SELF-ESTEEM

FIGURE 4. The Role of Employee Commitment in Trade

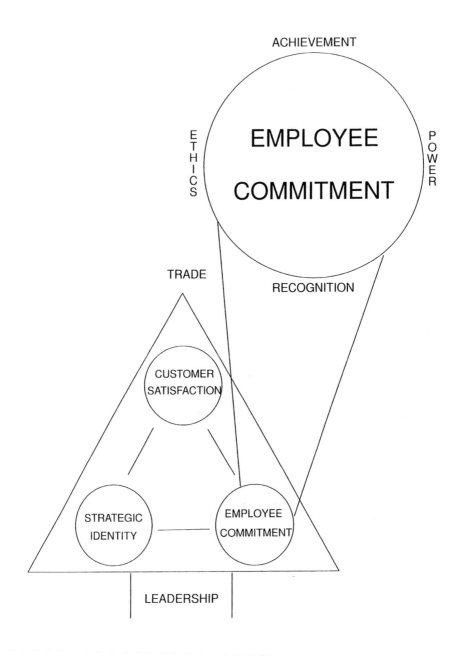

*The final test of a leader is that he leaves behind him in other men the conviction and the will to carry on.*

—Walter Lippmann

Self-esteem was the subject of my 1981 book published by Prentice-Hall. Now, many years later, the vital importance of self-esteem to performance and personal health is much more widely recognized. It receives regular mention in business journals, books, in some boardrooms, and even on radio programs. Unfortunately, the concept has been so popularized that its meaning and importance have become blurred.

Long before the book was published, consultants and researchers in our firm, universities, and elsewhere struggled with the meaning of self-esteem, for individuals and for organizations. Today there is widespread agreement that a positive sense of self-worth and value, of genuine self-confidence, is essential to continuing high levels of personal and organization performance. It is that simple and that difficult. The preceding figure illustrates the various factors affecting employee commitment and, thereby, personal and organizational performance.

There is in nearly all of us a powerful need to fundamentally approve of and like who we are. At our center, each of us needs to believe that we are powerful, effective, worthwhile, and competent. When people feel that way about themselves, including you and I, you can see it in their actions and hear it when they speak. It is true of young children and their parents and of employees and executives. With a positive sense of genuine self-respect and self-confidence, you and I meet life's challenges with assurance, anticipation, and confidence. We are likely to be more communicative, creative, energetic, and focused in important areas of our lives.

The reverse is also true. When we don't like ourselves, when we feel powerless, ineffective, and inadequate, our actions and words reflect that pain. Many will withdraw and retreat, becoming sad, brittle, and uninvolved. Energy, focus, and creativity plummet, and once satisfying activities and relationships no longer give much pleasure. These are among the devastating emotional and behavioral consequences of low self-confidence.

All of us have experienced periods of both high and low self-respect. Life and our own actions build up self-confidence, and tear it down. We have all known times of wonderful confidence when both the present and the future felt good, exciting, and even joyous. And we know the misery when today feels lousy and tomorrow seems bleak, depressing, and even frightening. All of these feelings mirror our self-esteem. So do our personal actions.

### Some Indicators of Positive Self-Esteem

1. Feel good, energetic, pro-active, worthwhile, self-responsible, confident, and sure.
2. Communicate openly and honestly, often and broadly, to and with many, at all levels.
3. State, confront, and resolve disagreement, opposition, and conflict: less concern with a "win" than with best solution.
4. Give to others: knowledge, ideas, encouragement, recognition. Share credit widely.
5. Find creative, new solutions and ways of looking at things.
6. Show sensitivity to needs, fears, and hopes of others.
7. Refrain from blaming others for problems; accept own responsibility.
8. Identify, diagnose, and propose solutions to problems. Deal well with change. Do not usually avoid or deny important issues.

These eight kinds of feelings and actions indicate just some of the typical and expected consequences of reasonably high, personal self-respect. Reverse all eight descriptions, and you have the consequences of low self-esteem. You have been there, and so have I.

We all know what high and low self-confidence does to our personal performance in most areas of our lives. When we feel good about who and what we are, our performance is also likely to be good. When self-confidence is low, performance will also be subpar. Self-respect is clearly a potent influence on personal feelings, actions, and performance. The following figure illustrates the relationship of self-esteem to performance.

Most people endlessly want something, some condition, that is more, better, or different. And always have. To get what we want, we must exchange something for what we want. What most of us have to trade is our time, energy, knowledge, and skill. The environments in which many such exchanges happen are the enterprises where our time, effort, and skills are exchanged for the money we use to make still more trades. But far more than money alone is part of the deal. Expectations about status, future opportunities, secure predictability, and fair treatment, among others, are less defined and often unspoken but equally real conditions of the trade and of the employment agreement.

Our work is usually much more than a factor in a purely financial transaction; it is a vehicle through which many other wants and needs

FIGURE 5. The Relationship Between Self-Esteem and Performance

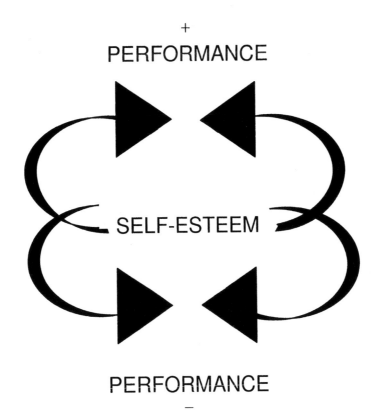

may be satisfied. For most, work is an exceedingly important part of our lives, true for a factory person and true for a senior-level professional or executive. To a significant degree our work is a defining component of who we are. The next time you are with some strangers, observe how many people ask "what do you do" or introduce themselves with some reference to where they work, their occupation, or job title.

Through work and the work environment, self-confidence can be very substantially increased or almost destroyed. Not exclusively through work, of course. Actions and events at home and elsewhere also have enormous impact on our sense of personal worth and value. And so, of course, did our early childhood experiences.

Even so, as adults a primary source of self-respect is the content of our work and the actions of people around us. The work environment holds numerous opportunities for measured achievement against goals and standards. There is evidence every day that we are valued, recognized, and cared about by customers, superiors, peers, and subordinates. Many of us find that we can influence and even control some important events and perhaps even direct the efforts of others. In the quality of our work and in how we treat others, there are frequent chances to act as our basic beliefs tell us we should.

When you ask people at all levels what makes them feel good or bad about their work, their positive replies tend to fall into one of four main categories:

1. Visible accomplishments and achievements toward valued, desired objectives; getting something done or at least making visible progress
2. Recognition and evidence of being cared about and valued by others; personal interest and attention; being favorably noticed
3. Influence, power, and control over choices, actions, and decisions, our own and those of others; freedom to choose and act
4. Behaving in ways that fit one's basic beliefs and values about work and other people; association with a company and individuals one believes are honest, decent, and honorable

The struggle to maintain and even increase confident feelings of personal worth and value begins very early in life. From then on, life and our own actions build up our self-respect and tear it down. Nearly everyone knows how it feels to be confident about our own competence and value, to ourselves and others. It is a joyous, optimistic, and affirmative experience that translates into vigorous, goal-oriented behavior on the job and in other important areas of our lives.

Nearly everyone also knows how lousy it feels when we don't like ourselves, when we don't feel valued, effective, or competent. It is a powerless, miserable experience when we look into ourselves and don't like what we see.

The focused energy of self-respect comes from success in the four primary areas described earlier. Continued failure in those same areas leads to low self-confidence, sadness, and even depression. Executives can dramatically influence which outcome is likely in the firms they lead.

Enhanced self-confidence from these four sources is at least potentially available to each of us in the context of the companies where we spend so much of our lives. Working largely alone can also offer opportunities for an expanded sense of self-worth and value. It may be more difficult simply because social and work interactions are more limited. At the same time, a solo entrepreneur of any kind has enormous autonomy and, most important, his or her achievements are almost immediately visible. Whether in a firm or working alone, all of us effectively trade skill and effort for money and also for at least the potential of increased self-respect.

Possibilities to improve self-confidence are all around us. They include relationships with family and friends, with one's supervisor, co-workers, and subordinates. There are nonvocational sources of self-esteem in hobbies, education, church, home, and civic activities. And, of course, there are many possibilities in the work environment: interests and challenges; visible achievements and advancement; freedom and access to information; inclusion, involvement, and influence; relationships and power.

Effective leaders know that all these conditions and more can add to commitment and effectiveness. They work to build firms where enhanced self-respect is available to many employees at all levels and from all four sources. They are adept at linking the four architectural components to opportunities for enhanced employee self-confidence. They know that sustained success in the market demands a level of focused concern and commitment available only to self-confident, assured people. There is nothing soft or altruistic about the driving motives and key decisions of such leaders, kind and considerate though most personally are. They know how dependent success is upon people who will selectively guide, accelerate, slow and deflect, the impact of change. When organization leaders deliberately establish and maintain conditions that permit employees to gain self-respect at work, those organizations tend to perform well over time and through periods of major transition.

Even dramatic changes in one or more of the four architectural elements will usually produce only short-term results if people do not wholeheartedly accept and buy in; or, worse, if such alterations actually reduce their self-confidence. People will invest themselves and make the commitment if it is clearly to their benefit to do so. Work conditions that enhance one's feelings of worth and value make the trade for greater commitment personally worthwhile even in times of great uncertainty and stress.

There are many examples of frozen pay levels, reduced benefits, longer hours, and even significant pay cuts that did not result in less employee commitment. The reason is that pay is only one aspect of what people trade their efforts to gain. The other, often more important consideration, is self-respect. After a certain income level, self-respect is substantially more important than money. Indeed, when reasonably compensated employees demand more money, it is often a consequence of low self-esteem, not economics.

Some recent independent research shows clearly that peoples' subjective well-being is largely independent of age, race, gender, and even income. It *is* associated with factors such as satisfying relationships, work achievements, a sense of personal control, and religious/spiritual commitment and values—the four components of self-esteem.

Self-respect is the linchpin between the individual, the four change levers available to leaders, and sustained organization performance. Threaten or damage it and even architectural changes essential to organization survival will have little positive effect. They may even make things worse.

Conversely, companies whose people enjoy a healthy sense of personal worth and value regularly overcome major barriers, including sometimes misguided management actions. When executive initiatives are well conceived, and member self-esteem is sound, organization leaders can expect exemplary performance. There are many important organizational consequences of either a prevailing positive or negative self-concept, as pictured in the following figure.

Companies, like individuals, are living systems; and, by analogy, the two share many processes. Entire firms sometimes seem to act in ways strikingly similar to the ways you and I might act as individuals whose confidence is high or low. For instance, you don't have to spend much time in a low-morale business unit to see and hear the following:

- Win or lose postures
- Blaming
- Intragroup conflict
- Anger, resentment
- Little joint problem solving
- Conflict avoidance
- "Telling and selling" communication patterns
- Autocratic management
- Little future orientation
- Low creativity
- Little self-responsibility
- Little risk taking
- Little commitment
- Parochialism
- Manipulation
- Politicking
- Mimicking a power figure
- One-way communication

These actions result, inevitably, in still further reduced company performance and in little satisfaction for either members or leaders.

The reverse is equally true. When people demonstrate a high level of confidence and an affirmative self-image, they demonstrate behaviors almost exactly opposite to those listed. They tend to perform very well indeed. In turn, individual members gain increased self-confidence from being a part of a winning organization, and the cycle spirals upward. At some visceral level, each of us knows the

FIGURE 6

# CONSEQUENCES OF SELF-ESTEEM

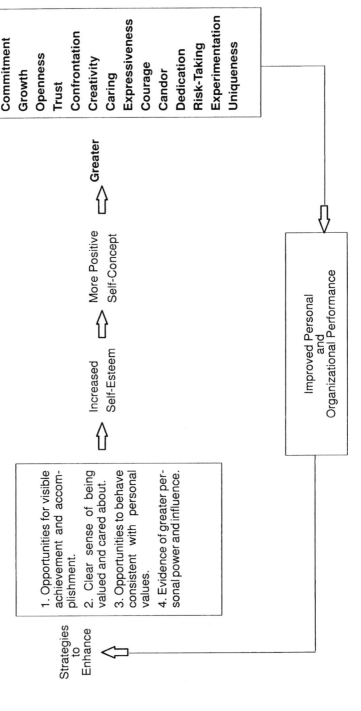

dramatic results of feeling good, or bad, about ourselves. We know what such feelings do for our effectiveness, energy, and performance.

Leaders can deliberately design and persistently pursue dozens of creative conditions that will enhance peoples' self-esteem at work. Sadly, a lot don't. Some will invest substantial assets in elaborate information systems and devise complex new differentiation strategies. Others may engage consultants to develop different organization structures or assign search firms to seek out new talent: all four architectural components may be vigorously engaged. These kinds of investments may be exactly what is needed. However, without an equally intense determination to make such changes in ways that preserve, protect, and even enhance employee commitment, the return is likely to be disappointing.

Jim Walker, head of AT&T's General Business Systems division pulled all four change levers. He did so over several years, and with very substantial input from all over the division. After some of the changes were in place, he and his key associate, Bill Davis, commissioned a study especially designed to show any misalignments or flaws. Then, he and his staff recalibrated, and readjusted, based on what people throughout the organization said.

Jim and Bill closely linked major architectural changes to the self-respect of key people everywhere in the division. They know that once you leave the "mahogany row" of executive offices, a company's traction force, its engine, is the self-confidence of people. Link architectural changes to member self-esteem and the probability of successful change rises dramatically.

There are four primary components of self-esteem. All are at least potentially available in the workplace, and all can be made much more so by management actions. Do so, and you materially add to the probability of successful trade. Capital multiplied by the efforts of committed people does equal trade.

# Chapter 9

# Achievement

People like to accomplish things they want to do or think are somehow worthwhile. It really is that straightforward. The ability to do so at work is remarkably infrequent for many managers and professionals. I have often observed that much of the often reported malaise in middle management results from an inability to achieve real outcomes or to experience the "lift" that comes from clear and visible accomplishment.

The positive feelings that come from achievement require that some risk and uncertainty be present. Achievement-oriented people are not dice rollers or gamblers: They want more control than that. Nor are they interested in risk-free "sure things" where there's no challenge and no self-satisfaction to be gained. They like to set goals and subgoals that they believe can be achieved with dedicated skill and effort. The lessons for leaders are clear. Together, *with* the people to be involved, do the following:

1. Select directions that are congruent and consistent with the firm's differentiation strategy and identity. Explain and show, again and again, how they fit.
2. Set difficult but reasonably achievable and, above all, specific standards and goals. Establish agreed-on success measures for the unit in terms of costs, quality, customer satisfaction, revenues and the like.
3. Develop a few transparent measures for each individual, department, or function. Keep the measures as simple and the comparisons as graphic as you can.
4. Provide necessary training, support, and coaching of any required skills. Provide for next stage, follow-up training.

Develop tests and certifications where appropriate. Training is a vital step and an initially expensive one.
5. Report accomplishment quickly, frequently, and visibly. Publicize and celebrate milestones.
6. Provide financial rewards for accomplishment.

It is clear from research and practice that many people can learn to be more achievement motivated. From my personal observation, people transferred into measurably higher achieving groups tend to become higher achievers themselves. Consider the following when transferring people or changing the firm's structure:

- Achievement motives can be measured and assessed. Yet relatively few firms have systems in place to deliberately select and hire such people throughout the organization. If the purposes of the company require achievement-oriented people, developing such selection systems would be a wise use of assets.
- For individual achievement desires to drive behaviors that are important to the company, there must be clear and objective outcome measures. How many of us would play golf if there was no way to measure ourselves (scoring systems) and no standard (par)? Developing achievement measures for as many individuals and groups as possible should be a higher priority than it usually is in most firms.
- If you want a particular kind of behavior or outcome, measure it. Then pay for achieving it. It is hard to think of a better way to use assets than to shape and reward measured performance. Except in sales, incentives clearly tied to measured outcomes are not very common in most firms.

Accomplishing visible, meaningful things *is* important to most of us. As an example, frontline employees and supervisors, especially in production-type environments, score significantly higher on achievement satisfaction questions than do middle-level managers and even senior specialists. When asked why, managers talk about useless paperwork, politics, and endless, nonproductive meetings. Frontline people speak proudly of increased sales, reduced cycle times, better product quality, lower costs, and fulfilled shipments, of finding real solutions to pressing problems. Even in paper and systems-intensive organizations, such as ADP, frontline people show genuine satisfaction with meeting a customer's needs, resolving knotty problems, or finding ways to improve the work process. The more that most people can improve their personal performance and their organization's outputs, the better they feel about themselves.

Achievements do not have to be public or grandiose to build self-esteem. A carpenter who worked on our new house described his obvious pride in a large deck he had just constructed.

> You'll notice that there's no give or sag. *I* know it's built right—the way it should be. Everything is cut right, fitted right and fastened right.

A representative at the bank I deal with took it as a personal challenge to fix an incredibly fouled up string of transactions. All I knew was that the statement was seriously incorrect. The representative was obviously proud to have figured out the multiple problems and fixed them.

The drive to achieve is strong enough that if there is little opportunity at work, many will develop hobbies and other outside skills and interests where visible achievement of desired goals is possible. Many working people undertake difficult courses of study to obtain additional knowledge and degrees. Others embark on arduous procedures to gain prestigious certifications. I know a metal sculptor who worked at no salary for an Air Products Corporation welder simply to learn technique. Can there be any doubt about the potency of the need to achieve?

This highlights three important conditions for achievement to positively impact self-esteem:

1. Goals and progress toward them must be visible to the people responsible. Gauges, charts, and graphs that show individual and small group performance against some expectation or past performance are ways of spotlighting achievement. There are many more. Pick just a few objectives, usually no more than three or four, and develop reliable systems to quickly report and show results.

2. The goals and objectives selected need to be desired by those responsible for achieving them. Meeting a standard you set for me provides much less "kick" than if it is a standard or goal I want to achieve. So, actively involve those responsible in determining the goals, standards, and measures.

3. To achieve the goals established, it is essential that those so charged have the required knowledge and skills. Otherwise, self-confidence is likely to suffer badly. For supervisors and managers, requisite knowledge and skills are often broader, but they are at least as important.

All too often, the education budget is the first to be cut when there are financial pressures, usually a serious error. Not only does such action reduce the likelihood of reaching important goals, it also clearly communicates that a remote management does not believe that the firm's people can contribute much to financial recovery and strength. By such action, management can actually reduce organization commitment and individual self-confidence just when both are needed most.

Goals of many kinds can serve as crossbars for achievement. Large scale interventions like total quality often involve mutually setting such objectives and providing sound, agreed upon measurements of progress in many different functional areas. For just a few examples, consider these:

*Operations:* reductions in measured defects per million parts; cost per unit; cycle time; scrap produced; energy consumed; late shipments; work in process.

*Accounting:* report reduction and elimination; greater accuracy; reduced report and closing cycle time; new indices; reduced receivables.

*Sales/Marketing:* measured customer satisfaction; order fill rate; market share; promotion effectiveness; advertising costs; new customers.

*Human Resources:* time to fill openings; workman's compensation claims; recruiting efficiency; grievances; training effectiveness.

We have found that people in particular functional areas or disciplines, at all levels, can develop and agree upon the most important measures—if they are invited and educated to do so. Often the people most immediately concerned know best what really counts and how to measure it. Ask them.

Definitions and measures of accomplishment and achievement are changing dramatically in many companies. For many managers and professionals, achievement has long been defined as a long succession of promotions through many grade levels to specifically desired titles or positions. Multilayered, highly structured organizations provide almost endless opportunity for this kind of movement, disguised as achievement, as do the static pay and job-grading systems so popular with corporate human resource departments.

The problem, of course, is that many companies are vigorously delayering by greatly reducing the number of different hierarchy levels and titles, and by moving toward more flexible approaches to pay and position. In many firms such once dependable goals and indicators of status, if not achievement, are much less available than only a decade ago. The increased incidence of temporary employment, more outsourcing, and the decline of secure predictability all mean that many people will come to define work accomplishment quite differently than their peers in more traditional hierarchies.

The need to achieve is strong in most of us. In staff and support groups, we frequently see talented people making great efforts to define for themselves achievement outcomes that are almost completely unimportant to organization success. Because there are typically few trade-relevant or measured results in such functions, people have defined achievement for themselves. They work very hard to leap those informally and consensually determined bars, so great effort is spent in competing for a private or larger office. Invitations to a higher status management meeting are coveted. A grander title, newer computer, or reserved parking space dominate thought and behavior. Sometimes middle-level managers describe their achievements in terms of full appointment calendars and lunch partners. None of these artificially determined accomplishments add much, if anything, to the organization's trading muscle.

It is also sad to see how little these artifices, so greatly desired, really add to individual self-respect. The personal impact is brief and, whatever positive feeling there may be, is entirely transient and individual. Some of these staff or support positions may add value, but many do not. A few present opportunity for real, measured achievement, but most do not.

In my observation, this malaise is not limited to any particular industry or type of company. It does appear to be more prevalent in multi-level, functionally structured, or bureaucratic organizations which have, in the past, been financially successful. Sometimes because of long ago, fortuitous positioning in a particular market.

Small-firm employees, and especially solos, have always described achievement in more measurable and individualistic ways. Cash flows, competitive success, new skills, professional recognitions, and new customers have considerable personal meaning to such people.

The task facing many large-firm leaders will increasingly be to define goals and accomplishments in more trade-relevant, less hierarchical or title-dependent ways. Most organizations define achievement in quite limited ways. But there are many possible ways to engage the drive for achievement and many more possible variations. The following list describes some of the ways to define and to set the bar height for achievement. In my experience, the most successful leaders try to clearly provide many avenues for accomplishment, not just a few standard or administrative routes.

1. Promotion to a genuinely more powerful position.
2. Lateral movement for deliberate, explained broadening and capability expansion.
3. Significantly larger-than-average pay raise.
4. Assignment to and service on important, high-visibility task forces or projects.
5. Being invited to set one's own goals, measures, and standards.
6. Time, or cycle time, reduction for any process, product, or output.
7. Elimination of steps, inspections, reports, parts, approvals.
8. Substitution of better or less expensive parts, systems, or processes of any kind.

9. Recognition from superiors and others—spot bonus, better office, time off; a personal "thanks" or a positive letter in personnel file—for specific accomplishment or action.
10. Posted, "public" scores or other measures of output, that compare the performance of one's unit vs. that achieved by others, or to past results of one's own unit.
11. Successfully closing down divested, or otherwise unnecessary functions, operations, offices, and facilities.
12. Selling assets, including technology and facilities.
13. Negotiating agreements with union, suppliers, governmental agencies.
14. Meeting or beating sales quotas.
15. Selling new or additional business.
16. Getting an incentive check for measured accomplishments.

Think about an organization you know reasonably well. How is achievement defined and measured? Are measured achievements clearly linked to the firm's ability to trade successfully? Does everyone know what these achievement expectations are? What other desired behaviors or outcomes could serve as organizationally and personally important results?

After a time, many people in a particular organization environment come to define themselves and their sense of personal worth and value largely in terms defined by that specific environment. Their self-esteem can become tightly attached to and dependent on the firm and membership in it. This occurs because the prevailing definitions of achievement, influence, recognition, and expressed beliefs have gradually become accepted as one's own. The organizations where so many of us spend our lives are important definers of what accomplishment is and how power can be acceptably gained and expressed. They specify what forms of personal recognition and caring will be tolerated and encouraged. And they often, though subtly, inculcate a variety of strong values and beliefs in their long-term members.

All of this was part of the unspoken contract between the person and the organization. Barring major difficulty, employees who accepted and internalized these cultural truths could generally depend on a secure berth. This remains true in many organizations, of course, but in many others it is changing painfully and dramatically.

When people, systems, asset use, and the organization itself change substantially, once dependable sources of self-respect become risky, uncertain, and tenuous. The resulting fear leads many to seek reassurance and definition about what achievement really *is* in the new environment. What is accepted; what is valued; what is safe when the ground shifts?

People who are dismissed during a downsizing, for instance, at least have a new chance to redefine themselves and to discover new sources of self-confidence from achievements they decide are worthwhile. Those who survive often remain enmeshed in a murky world of shifting expectations, still dependent on unreliable, antique definitions of achievement for personal identity and self-respect. Leaders of changing companies have no more important responsibility than to crisply define what achievement means and what accomplishments will be valued in the new environment.

Close behind the responsibility to define and clarify desired achievement is the requirement to provide people with appropriate skills, responsive systems to track and reward accomplishment, and organization structures and processes to enable real achievement. Major change violently disrupts the once-clear definitions and self-confidence that are essential to renewed health of the firm. Successful transitions demand the use of far more assets for a longer time than most leaders realize at the outset. Every executive I know who has led his company through major, dislocating change of any kind agrees that it always costs much more than you expect.

A manufacturing vice president, who championed and led a textbook TQM (Total Quality Management) initiative, concurs:

> I talked to a lot of people before we started. I squirrelled away about twice the money I thought we'd need. Boy was I wrong! The payback has been much larger and even faster than we forecast, but the front-end costs were enormous. You bet I'd do it again in a minute. But I'd get hold of a lot more money before starting.

I view as ultimately healthy the disintegration of the old, paternalistic contract between employee and employer. That psychologically dramatic change now seems to be accompanied by the early stages of a related breakdown of similarly paternalistic expectations between citizens and government. How far the second change will extend is anyone's guess. The first is well underway and continuing at a brisk rate. There remain, though, many leaders who have yet to seriously consider the kind of employer-employee relationship that will add to the firm's long-term trading ability. There are still large cadres of powerless and dependent middle-level managers who are at considerable risk.

Any large company professional employee above, say, first or second level supervisor or below general manager or vice president, should consider all realistic options and alternatives well before the decision is made by others. The fact is that each of us is ultimately and alone responsible for our individual sense of personal worth and value. No one and no institution can give self-confidence to anyone. But that is the silent fiction accepted by millions of professional employees for decades. It has been part of the informal contract that is now without much remaining foundation.

# Chapter 10

# Recognition and Being Valued

From birth onward all of us have needed the caring of others to survive: physically, during our earliest days and emotionally, for the rest of our lives. Being clearly valued, recognized, and cared about is a primary source of self-confidence. The need for approval and recognition from others drives an enormous range of human behavior in every area of activity. Often, actions explained as arising from some other motive are actually efforts to gain self-respect through the approval, respect, and caring of others.

You may know people who appear to exert extraordinary effort at work; they are in early and out late. Their cars are in the company parking lot on weekends. Such dedication might be driven by a commitment to some consuming project or goal, or by a need to achieve. Or it may reflect a need to attract the attention, notice, and approval of important officials. I have met managers who say they have obtained the schedules of senior executives for just that purpose.

We all know others who work hard to become significant figures in their profession, their church, civic groups, or in the public arena. Published articles, research, and patents provide recognition for still others. Many hobbies can be vehicles for praise and notice as well. We all need evidence of being noticed, valued, and recognized by others.

I've met two mayors of small towns whose management careers were probably secure but also routine and tedious. One was a controller, the other a personnel manager. Both found challenge and renewed self-confidence in their elected roles.

> Its fun. I'm in the middle of everything, and my opinion is asked a lot more than it is at the plant. Every day I meet with important business and political people I'd never even see in my plant job.

Most people spend a large proportion of their lives in a workplace, trading time, energy, and skills for money and for self-respect. The workplace abounds in opportunities to feel valued, cared about, and recognized as a worthwhile human being. From co-workers in one's area and the person in the next office, to companions in the cafeteria and still others who gather in meetings, the workplace is a rich milieu of formal and informal supportive relationships. Among the most important commitment builders are positive expressions of approval from one's boss or others in authority positions. Interest and caring by co-workers is another. When the quality of those relationships and exchanges is generally positive and supportive, self-confidence is enhanced. Leaders are usually wise to deliberately provide many opportunities for such positive interchanges. Beer busts, extended cafeteria lunch hours, and employee interest/hobby groups are examples.

Certainly, both formal and less formal organization policies and practices can contribute to feelings of being valued and cared about. Benefit plans, child care, insurances, and worklife quality initiatives of many kinds serve this purpose. They show that company leaders are interested in employee concerns. Even infrequently used provisions, such as tuition reimbursement, will be cited by hourly people, managers, and professionals alike as evidence that company leaders truly care. In smaller firms, especially, birthday cards personally signed by the president or owner(s) are welcomed and often displayed.

Sometimes special, out-of-policy, actions can be potent demonstrations that one is valued. In the early 1960s, I was promoted and transferred from a low cost-of-living area to New York City. During the transfer, my wife suddenly became seriously ill, so I had to make several sudden trips back home. Understand, please, that despite the coveted promotion and pay increase, our financial condition was awful.

At the conclusion of the transfer process, when things had settled somewhat, my supervisor, Tom, and his boss, a senior offical, took me aside. Tom did the talking. Very quietly he said:

> I expect you lost a lot while making this transfer. I want to see three or four expense reports that cover your loss. Wash it, eat it, travel it. Whatever. Be creative. We don't expect you to make money, but you damn sure shouldn't lose.

His superior just nodded. The process was demonstrably counter to dozens of authoritative, corporate directives. Clearly, I was cared about and would have done anything for such men and such a company.

Even more important to self-respect than frequent, informal, peer contacts are those authority relationships shown on the organization charts. Being recognized and valued for one's importance, contribution, and competence by those of greater knowledge, power, and authority is a definite boost to almost anyone's confidence. True for a company president praised by the board of directors, and true for an engineer recognized by the branch manager. We never outgrow our need to be recognized and appreciated. Properly designed, performance-appraisal systems that encourage genuine dialogue can positively impact self-esteem. Some personnel departments are structured to provide competent, caring counsel to employees. Employee assistance programs are typically contracted to outside agencies professionally staffed to help employees with drug, alcohol, and other problems.

The most effective leaders I know, regardless of hierarchy level, exert considerable effort to know who has contributed above and beyond, and they take every opportunity to let the individual know that they know, both face to face and indirectly. Such executives not only build the self-respect of others, they gain in stature and influence themselves. Hard to find a better trade. Surprisingly few leaders realize how truly powerful they can be in enhancing the self-confidence and, thereby, the performance of others.

Direct praise for superior contribution and genuine appreciation for difficult problems faced and overcome clearly shows caring and recognition. Bob Correll, Duracell's top executive for product quality, is a master. Bob regularly travels to all Duracell plants, laboratories, and offices. He possesses a razor-sharp mind, a thoroughly detailed system, and a memory that records the activities, achievements, and difficulties confronted by just about everyone he's likely to meet. It is worth the trip to watch Bob greet a bunch of engineers, supervisors, and managers. He works his way one by one to selected individuals. In a voice both quiet and intense, he offers high praise and professional understanding. The impact on the individuals and the company is enormous. They've told me so.

Bud Agner, Senior Vice President of Mercury Marine, regularly walks through the company's huge manufacturing plants. Because he's also a fully trained toolmaker, when Bud stops to talk, everyone listens. He's entirely capable of rolling up his sleeves and showing someone how to make a difficult setup. He doesn't have time to do it very often, but when he does, it is widely known in minutes. In very different ways, both executives demonstrate an intense, personal level of caring and recognition.

Another way of demonstrating caring and recognition is asking someone to help or contribute to the solution of some important problem as illustrated by the following quotation from an interview with a young manager:

> You could have knocked me over. The old man, a vice president, comes in my office. Hell, I don't see him once a month. He said . . . Sam, come with me. You don't know anything about this problem, but you have good judgment.

Later he said:

> Damn, that felt good. I worked awful hard and long to help fix that, in addition to running my own department.

Every employee and every group of employees is a large, and largely underutilized, expert resource. There is no better way to engage the committed energy of people than to value and openly recognize those who can and do contribute.

Allen Fleischer, CEO of PepCom Industries, does this exceptionally well. Allen requests and receives frequent reports of extraordinary effort and performance by PepCom people in all facilities. Within a week, or two at the most, Allen visits the facility. Both privately and publicly he praises the individual responsible.

The news doesn't always have to be good to be an opportunity for an expression of confidence-building. I was present some years ago when a senior engineer sadly reported to the CEO and his staff that a costly, new prototype had failed completely. One or two people began to raise some questions that sounded very much like the start of blame. The CEO interrupted:

> I've followed this one. Charlie here and his team did everything reasonable and then some. They did a damn good job. In

our business you sometimes fail spectacularly. I know I have. Charlie, you and your people take a day or two off. Then let's get together and see how we can pull this together. Tell everyone thanks from me for all their work. And I meant it, Charlie. You did damn well with something we all knew was high risk.

One clear way to recognize contribution is through concrete, financial incentives, as discussed earlier. But concrete incentives do not have to be directly financial. There are dozens of ways leaders at all levels can provide evidence of caring and valuing. In a union and some other environments, it may require creativity and entail some modest risk, but it can be done.

Many years ago a young production supervisor in a unionized facility kept a number of six-packs of beer in the trunk of his car. It was never locked. When one or another of the people in the group contributed exceptionally, he or she was invited to "stop by the car" after clocking out. No one ever took more than one six-pack. Everything done in this situation was grounds for dismissal, but it was a potent way to show tangible appreciation for outstanding effort and work. The unit performed exceptionally, and the supervisor thought the risk acceptable. In this deeply religious community, the same supervisor attended a good many funerals held for relatives of his people. A small thing, perhaps, but a clear expression of caring and concern.

One executive in a software company uses his deep, informal contacts every few months to find the name of someone doing exceptional work. He casually wanders into that employee's work area and offers fulsome, public praise. The impact reaches far beyond the employee; the grapevine quickly spreads the news.

There are almost limitless, nonfinancial ways to show people that they are valued. Providing timely, accurate information to every person in the place is one of the best, and one of the most underutilized. Small group conversations with an executive is another. Management presence at important employee milestone events is also a powerful demonstration of caring and valuing. Judicious breaking of rules and standards for selected people and for the "right" reason can send a powerful signal of caring and concern throughout the organization.

Clearly, a senior leader or executive in a large organization has a limited personal "reach." But he or she can establish clear expectations with subordinate managers. The personal "reach" of the senior executive can be extended by something as simple as a call to the individual's boss or a short, personal conversation. One CEO sends brief but specific notes by company e-mail. There are many more possibilities.

Among the unavoidable casualties of continuous downsizing and restructurings are important work relationships and the self-esteem that results from them. The sense of belonging, cohesion, and shared experience that so many gain from work often does not survive such change. It is not only those dismissed who suffer a loss of self-esteem. Employees who remain often experience considerable guilt, sadness, and a nagging anxiety. In such a climate, it is not uncommon for survivors to report that they have pulled back and partly withdrawn from previously important work relationships, interests, and commitments. The sense of organization identity and "we feeling" declines and along with it individual self-confidence and organization vitality. Wise executives will see to it that employees selected to survive a reorganization know, beyond question, that they are the carefully selected and strongly valued cadre on whom the leader depends. If survival of the enterprise or other clearly evident threat requires radical restructuring, be as open and candid as you can legally be. Leaders who attempt to mask or disguise an inevitability that everyone already suspects will destroy their ability to lead effectively.

I know one printing industry executive forced to radically downsize. He and his key people somehow reached every remaining supervisor with the message ". . . you're the best. I rely on you. Come see me any time." A new sense of cohesion, mutual confidence, and self-respect gradually developed, and the firm survived.

The lesson is clear. If employees must be dismissed, first eliminate functions, plants, departments, and activities that do not clearly contribute to trade. Second, select and strongly assure those key people at all levels whom you must retain to succeed. Above all, keep your word. Only then begin the layoff process. In this way, supportive relationships will more quickly develop, so that people can regain a sense of importance and the firm its identity. Under such conditions, it is probably not possible to overcommunicate or to provide too many opportunities for personal contact among people in various functions and hierarchy levels. There is always a lot of pain, sadness, and fear that will dissipate better if people can talk and share their feelings.

It also seems likely to me that the increase in outsourcing entire functions, and of hiring temporary employees, will also tend to reduce cohesion, company identity, and loyalty. Who, exactly, is the "we" when many co-workers are temporary and when important functions are contracted to outsiders? This will be an expanding problem for leaders, their subordinates, and also for the outside contractors and temporary employees themselves. Their self-respect is unlikely to be enhanced by the kinds of caring relationships available to the permanent staff. Managers of such temporary people will need to exert extra effort and attention to sustain their commitment and performance. Similarly, a vigorous acquisition-divestiture strategy, with resulting frequent changes in people and organization, can further distance employees from the company, its leaders, and each other. The result is likely to be less self-confidence and less commitment to company success.

Yes, leaders will be wrong. Events they cannot foresee or control will inevitably mean that some reassured, strongly desired people do not remain. In my view, uncertainty is not an acceptable excuse for adopting a remote, uncaring, or distant posture in times of painful turmoil. It is precisely under these conditions that we see who the real leaders are. Showing that you care, especially during times of radical change, demands considerable time, energy, and thoughtfulness. There are few better investments.

# Chapter 11

# Power, Control, and Influence

*The highest proof of virtue is to possess boundless power without abusing it.*

—Macaulay

It is in the nature of people to want to control their environment and what goes on in it. With evidence of personal influence and power come the feelings of self-assurance and confidence that are essential to top performance. People with little self-respect cannot perform well or handle changing conditions effectively. All of us want to control, or at least substantially influence, the people, conditions, and events around us. We want some power of choice and some freedom to decide for ourselves. Examples are everywhere. My wife never stops reconfiguring our property by rearranging the trees and shrubs. A retired associate likes to build wonderful stone walls, planters, and grottos on his land. A business-owner friend decided to enter local politics and has been elected three times to city council. All of these represent the efforts of individuals to direct, decide, influence, and control some part of their environment.

The ethical pursuit of power, influence, and control is entirely legitimate. One important way to increase one's influence and control is to trade for what we want. Whether what I want is a particular thing, like a car, or more education, a better job, or anything else, I must trade for it. I exchange money, time, energy, and skill or something else I possess for something I want. Politicians barter time, inconvenience, money, and promises for the chance to exercise more influence. Executives and other people, too, exchange comfort, time, skills, and other considerations for higher-level positions that promise greater power and control over the direction of the department, one's career, or even the company. Entrepreneurs swap security for autonomy and a chance to pursue their own dream.

Most of us don't like to have anything important done *to* us by others because that shows that we have little control. It violates our need for influence and power. I suspect a great many lawsuits are undertaken less for demonstrable hurt and damage than for "they can't do that to me" reasons. We once advised a hospital to put telephones back into rooms occupied by recovering senior executives and professionals. The absence of telephones told these control-oriented patients that they had no influence. The change was credited with reducing hospital stays by several days. Having no influence or control can literally make you sick! Many business process redesign efforts fail because people believe, often correctly, that things are being done *to* them, and in ways that make it clear that they have no power, control, or influence. At best, sullen acceptance and at worst, active sabotage are common outcomes.

The desire for personal control is precisely why strategies like enriched jobs, total quality, decentralization, and self-managed work groups often work out so well. Such strategies deliberately put power and control into the hands of more people, the performing people who know best what needs to be done and how to do it.

In return for greater personal control, one is usually expected to assume greater personal responsibility, risk, and accountability for his or her actions. That's the deal. Some will like it, others will not. People vary considerably in the amount of influence they want in their work and particularly in the level of risk they are willing to assume to get it. A frequent mistake by leaders is to assume that everyone wants as much control as they, and is willing to pay as much. Many people say they want the power; far fewer are really willing to make the trade.

Careful initial design, selecting the right people, and day-to-day attention to risks and rewards are required for successful work enrichment and self-managed group strategies to succeed. Those who are willing to assume some risk in return for a greater measure of control usually like such innovations and perform very well. Others may greatly fear the consequences of a bad choice or decision and will prefer a traditional management approach. Increased freedom and influence is not for everyone or every firm.

During twenty-five years as an advisor to executives and managers, dozens of highly skilled people have said to me, "I'm going to leave this [company, law firm, clinic, etc] and go on my own." In those twenty-five years, only a few have done so. For most, the deal was too unbalanced. Potential control was wonderful to contemplate, too risky to pursue.

When moving toward true, stand-alone business units, toward total quality or self-managed work groups, for instance, it is vital to carefully design the environment, select the people, and provide the training and education required. It simply can't be done without the commitment of substantial assets. Organization processes and structures, various systems and people, will probably need to change. Don't expect quick results. Performance will almost certainly decline somewhat before it turns decidedly positive, as it very likely will. In our experience, well-considered, self-managed groups succeed over 70 percent of the time, as do work-enrichment and other genuinely inclusive and empowering initiatives, if supported over some years. They are all conceptually and psychologically quite similar because they enhance self-respect and, therefore, performance. But they are decidedly not for everyone or every leader.

In the late 1970s, Rexnord Corporation moved aggressively toward true, stand-alone business units from decades of near total, top-down centralization. Rexnord's chairman and CEO saw to it that considerable funds would be available to, essentially, recreate Rexnord's identity into something quite different. Bob Kidon and Phil Browne, the key personnel and organization executives, knew that careful redefinition of leader roles, new reporting systems, careful executive selection, and very substantial education would be required. The dramatic transition to a decentralized structure and new organization was among the smoothest and most effective I have seen, and the financial outcomes were gratifying. Even so, it took several years.

Our need for control and influence is strong. In dozens of employee opinion and attitude surveys, in a range of industries, this need is usually shown to be significantly unmet in the work environment. The difference between the desired and experienced level (of influence) is larger for this need than for the others measured. The gap, or deficit, is often largest for hourly employees though it is not much smaller for supervisors and middle managers. If needs for a desired measure of power and control are thwarted by the official or formal work environment, they will often be met informally.

For instance, people will often control their work commitment and output to a level they think is fair or reasonable. Professional and management employees can readily reduce their hours of contribution during the workweek or on weekends. They can easily, and almost invisibly, reduce commitment, energy, and activities. They can reduce their side of the usually unspoken employment equation to a level they think makes the trade fair. By doing so, they gain a significantly increased degree of power and control. Ultimately, they can leave altogether—an expression of complete control over that particular situation.

In factory and some office settings, there are usually unofficial "banks" of materials, products, and tools. These "banks" are informal inventions set aside by workers against an expected future management failure or requirement. The employees bend the formal system to gain some control.

When I was a young, factory supervisor in a union plant many years ago, upper management suddenly levied greatly increased output requirements that just could not be met. There was not enough material on the line or in the storerooms. The career threat from my autocratic boss was clearly stated. I shared the problem openly with the senior hourly people in my group, more in frustration than in any expectation of reprieve. These four or five people unexpectedly appeared together at my desk that afternoon and urged me to take a long walk around the thirty-acre plant. There wasn't much to lose, so I did.

Upon my return, dozens of already inspected, completed products were moving smoothly down the line. There were lots of very broad smiles and winks from people in the group. They had emptied the "bank" for me, a bank I had not known existed. The "bank" and the complex processes required to build it were effective ways for them to gain power and control in an impersonal, line-speed and schedule-driven factory environment. By using the "bank" to help me, they demonstrated a considerable amount of control, far more than upper management ever imagined.

As I later came to understand, the primary purpose of the "bank" was to maintain a smooth production flow. It served to maintain the level of piecework incentive pay when individuals or subgroups had a "bad" day because of upstream process failures, unavailable parts, or simple mistakes. A second-order outcome of the bank was that downstream inspection, packing, and shipping groups had a more steady in-flow of products. I suppose it is possible that the "bank" also helped assure that our customers' needs would be met on schedule.

In both office and factory environments, I have been told of hidden, banked resources much of the time. While such activities certainly increase people's sense of control and self-respect, consider the implications for the firm's other functions and its formal reporting and control systems, such as purchasing or inventory control.

Managers and professionals who feel powerless usually have more alternatives than factory workers, though not always. Through broader experiences and more formal education, professionals have wide networks of friends and associates. They can circulate résumés and more readily change jobs, companies, industries, and even countries. Those with especially powerful desires for control and autonomy may accept the risks of leaving their employer to establish their own company. Yes, there is an array of alternatives for people to gain influence at work. From work slowdowns, passing on rumors, and politicking with superiors; to leaking information, withdrawing time and energy, and departing to another organization, people will seek to meet their needs for influence, power, and control because it is vital to their self-esteem.

The traditional large company pyramid with its many titles and levels was and is ideally structured to provide the appearance of progressively greater power and control. Many people measure their corporate lives, personal success, and careers by promotions from one level to the next. That many such titles and assumed advancements are largely artificial and of minimal real consequence does not matter. For many of us, our sense of who we are is tightly tied to the believed prominence of the company and our own position within it.

For many employees, radical delayering, spin-offs, and downsizings have greatly reduced the opportunity for increased position power. While it is certainly true that flattening and decentralizing have strengthened the ability of many organizations to trade, the fact is that there are fewer steps on the power ladder. And that, in turn, poses a leadership problem in companies that have long depended on a multi-step, hierarchy structure for motivation and reward. Instituting radically different ways to reward contribution and to confer increased power will prove to be even more revolutionary than the precipitating organization realignments, dramatic as many have been.

The impact of restructurings on member self-confidence has been and will continue to be substantial. People will search out new ways of demonstrating to themselves and others that they have appropriate amounts of control and influence. In one company, top management has tried for three years to eliminate nearly all job titles. Everyone is an "associate." The intent is to enhance communication and accessibility. It has not worked. Informally, the old titles remain in everyday use, and relationships are still largely guided by the presumed influence and control of the person in each position. Cosmetic changes, even in the service of a worthy goal, can not often overcome the need to exercise power ourselves or the desire to respond appropriately to it in others.

For the thousands of managers and professionals laid off from large and small firms, the separation has often been a terrible blow to personal identity and self-esteem. Not though, for financial reasons alone, because the severance packages have often been generous. Dismissal removes a once predictable and visible source of personal influence and also one's secure position in a dependable web of power relationships.

For people whose sense of identity and self-respect is inseparable from organization indicators of influence, the impact has been especially severe. They have the task of redefining their lives and careers to permit adequate esteem income from other sources. Nor is the impact limited to those actually dismissed. Regardless of title, many employees who remain often begin to seriously question their own real influence and level of personal control over events. If peers and even superiors can be dismissed, I may have no control at all over what will happen to me.

And so we see huge numbers of résumés from talented, presently employed people seeking new venues. We read of increasing numbers of new business ventures. Both seem to me healthy signals that people are taking charge and redefining their sense of self-and worth.

## THE DEPOWERING OF MIDMANAGEMENT

Fifteen years ago our research began to show that perceived powerlessness and loss of personal control was deeply troubling to many employees. The results were the same in company after company and at all hierarchy levels, except at the very top.

Not long ago, the power to make changes, to decide, and to spend company money correlated strongly with hierarchy level. Factory and office people had very little power, and without prior approval could take little independent action. Middle-level managers in many firms were relatively influential. They could often make personnel and organization changes themselves and could frequently approve the spending of appreciable funds. At the minimum, these managers could and did greatly impact the decisions of senior leaders. It is a generalization, of course, but the relatively linear relationship between hierarchy position and power seems to be changing dramatically in many companies. Today we often find a bimodal distribution of power.

For instance, lower-positioned people may now have considerable ability to make significant changes and to decide, though not often, to spend company money without approval. Empowered work groups, the SMGs discussed earlier, frequently decide work flow, work schedules, and job assignments along with quality and discipline standards. In some cases they appoint or elect their own leaders and are often asked for spending recommendations. Asset use, people, the organization itself, and important systems have all changed in such firms.

Senior leaders, typically vice presidents and above, have great autonomy, decision authority, and the power to spend significant company money. Final authority rests at the top of the hierarchy, whether relatively flat or tall, just as it always has.

The dramatic change is in the middle. People with titles like manager, senior manager, and director are often largely powerless and without much influence. They have become workers and lone contributors. Not long ago, people with such titles could often direct significant change in the structure of their functions or departments. They approved sizable contracts with outside vendors, made hiring and promotion decisions, and caused the purchase or internal redesign of important business systems. They were leaders in fact, not just by title. To a significant degree, the power and influence that once accompanied a managerial title now reside with vice presidents. As a result, it is not uncommon to see a senior executive's desk burdened with files of requests for decisions that a few years ago would long since have been resolved at lower levels. Because senior executives have other responsibilities and simply can not personally know whether the requests are sound, decisions and actions about important internal issues are increasingly slow and often very risky. Some companies and their leaders seem to be frozen in place as a blizzard of unresolved problems and decisions piles up at their door. While senior-executive energy and attention is focused on high-level, often external issues, internal processes slow, except at the "floor" or working level.

Whether a result of formal restriction or a consequence of fear and job insecurity, many middle managers in large companies are little more than expediters, coat holders, or, more positively, individual contributors. Relatively few are gaining the kind of guided experiences with complex problem-analysis and decision-making that were important skills to their predecessors a decade ago. The gap between the executive suite and the productive part of the company has grown wider, a consequence of fewer, and especially less active and influential middle managers who linked the two.

In quantitative research in dozens of companies, in every year since our earliest studies, the same problem of low individual influence has emerged as primary, and it has become ever more so. Indeed, the issue of power, influence, and control seems to be an increasingly important factor in the way people feel about federal, state, and local governments as well as their own employment situation.

Recently, voters here rejected a bond issue for the school system. That has happened only once before. The predictable pattern has been for respected community leaders to vigorously promote general-obligation, school bonds, and for voters to overwhelmingly approve them and the higher taxes required. Not this time. One reason was a lot of individual voter decisions to regain control and to exercise influence.

Many people are deciding to leave the corporate world for small-firm, temporary, or self-employment. Behind many such decisions is the issue of power and powerlessness, personal control and individual influence. Precisely the same concern has driven the formation of many powerful, citizen-action and other influential groups. It is all about personal power, control, and influence. I believe this is and will increasingly be the central issue to confront leaders in the future in most kinds of institutions.

Wise leaders establish conditions so that such powerful needs can be met in the work environment. The following initiatives are among those that have been successful. They have helped refine and redefine company identities and thereby resulted in firms more able to trade successfully.

*Work/job enrichment*—adding substantive decision authority to jobs at all levels and in all functions.

*Self-managed work groups* in offices, manufacturing plants, and laboratories.

*Cross-functional* task teams of many kinds—temporary teams created to solve important problems.

*Employee ownership* (ESOPs). Where "real" ownership is not available, phantom stock plans and joint ventures have proven useful.

*Operator verification* of own work. Some leading firms no longer have the large inspection departments that were once common.

*Incentive compensation* systems of many kinds. Several have been described earlier.

*Flat hierarchies* and other "ease of access" methods such as smaller organization units, informality, and leader availability approaches.

*Training and education* opportunities. Knowledge *is* power; so can be the close, productive relationships that often result. Training is a primary requirement for successful change.

*Team development* is a specific kind of education that is a necessary condition for many group-focused interventions like self-managed groups.

*Cross-training* used to be common and should be again: people with more skills are more self-confident, and are able to contribute in a larger variety of situations.

*Skunk works.* Get a few people together, organize yourselves and try it out; usually works best when allowed to function largely independent of the rest of the firm.

*Assignment choices.* Some leaders carefully select a few people and allow them the power to choose or even create their next position.

*Multilevel,* multifunction participation and inclusion can be the basis for much stronger teamwork and commitment, companywide.

*Promotions.* The traditional, and still important, way of granting more power and influence.

*Total quality* management—but only if top management personally partakes of the training and actively "walks the talk." ISO certification processes often serve a similar purpose and have similar requirements.

Few leaders or their companies can employ all of these. Most can very successfully engage two or three if assets are committed, the effort is carefully matched to the prevailing culture, and there is top-leader focus for several years. None will accomplish much if adopted as a short range, fad-of-the-month tactic. Methods such as these are not soft or easy strategies. Fully embraced, they can build employee self-confidence, better satisfy customers, and thereby increase the organization's ability to trade successfully.

Of the four sources of self-esteem described in this book, none provides as much organization leverage as increased power and influence. I suspect the reason is that the gap between the level of influence people want and what they experience is the largest for this factor.

This is especially true in anxious times of change and uncertainty. All too often we see leaders of threatened companies increas-

ingly attempt to gather all power into the executive suite in an effort
to exercise ever tighter control. This may temporarily relieve the
leader's fear, but it usually prolongs the decline of trade and retards
recovery. Wise leaders somehow know that the way power works is
counterintuitive: with power, the more you give away, the more you
have. That is why in times of stress these same wise leaders are apt
to begin or accelerate initiatives to push power down into the organization where productive people will use it to increase trade. It
takes considerable courage. The process entails risk and demands
commitment. Most often, it works.

This does not mean that such effective leaders have in any way lost
stature or authority. They vigorously use all four of the change levers
including the divestiture of organization units, downsizing, or pay
reductions. But they also seek ways to increase the influence of individuals and units that remain. They know that recovery ultimately
requires the effort of confident, committed people with healthy levels
of self-esteem. In the process, such executives tend to gain considerable personal standing.

# Chapter 12

# Validating Beliefs and Values

Somewhere near the center of most of us are some strongly held beliefs and values against which we test ourselves and others. The power of belief can be enormous. Throughout history, millions of people have willingly died in the service of fiercely held beliefs. Religions, nations, political parties, and many more institutions have been founded and maintained to advance and protect one or another system of shared beliefs. Values and beliefs are powerful because they are so central to personality that they are often not identified or obvious. They usually operate in the background, directing attention and guiding behavior.

There are two reasons why our core values and beliefs are of great practical importance. First, belief systems act like filters and lenses. All of us interpret events, including the actions of ourselves and others, through the filter of our beliefs about what is right or wrong, proper or improper. Two people can observe exactly the same event or hear the same words. One individual responds very favorably, the other reacts just as negatively. Without always knowing why, we quickly evaluate events as good or bad, fair or unfair, decent or morally repugnant. The filter of beliefs typically operates very quickly, often without our even being consciously aware of it. Not only does the value filter operate quickly, but because they are so central to who we are, value-based judgments tend to be very certain and very strong. The more central the value or belief, the faster and stronger the evaluation, whether positive or negative. Beliefs strongly influence what we perceive and how we respond.

A second reason that values and beliefs are practically important is that they act like an unconscious compass. They often demand action, focus our attention and motivate specific behavior in many situations. Often we are not even aware of why we act as we do. The most typical behavioral response is to move toward or away from a situation that engages our core values and beliefs. In that sense, values and beliefs are efficient. They direct our attention, evaluation, and behavior so that we do not need to consciously think through every situation we confront.

Values and beliefs are core parts of who we are. They have much to do with how we interpret and evaluate what is going on in the environment. They can cause us to respond and act almost automatically. Our values and beliefs are truly relentless dictators.

Acting in ways that fit and validate our beliefs and core values adds to personal self-respect. When we behave as our values and sense of ethics require, we feel strong and virtuous; we approve of and like ourselves. Whenever we act counter to those basic beliefs, we don't like ourselves. We feel guilty, remorseful, and worthless. Most people try to avoid individuals or organizations they believe to be basically dishonest or unethical. Acting as our values demand adds to our self-confidence and sense of self-respect. Associating with others who share our beliefs confirms our own worth and value.

Recently we have all read of serious legal charges and some guilty pleas by over twenty Honda USA executives. They have apparently been part of a decade-long process of bribery and corruption. All this was suspected by some of our dealer clients who refused to have anything to do with Honda during a time when a Honda franchise was a guarantee of wealth. One well-known dealer told me in 1985 or 1986, "My name, the reputation of this dealership, and the honest people who work here would all be hurt by any association with Honda. I want nothing to do with that crowd."

Could there be a clearer example of the power of values to direct attention and motivate behavior? A lot of honest Honda employees at all levels have probably been hurt and deeply offended by the revelations.

A major airline recently fired an employee I know for jostling, without damage, a parked airliner. His tractor was hooked up to the plane prior to pushing it back for takeoff. He says that the brakes on his tractor and on others were faulty because of efforts to reduce maintenance costs. I believe him, and so do his co-workers. They say the company now tries to blame all its problems on lower-level people rather than on misguided management actions. The perceived dishonesty has embittered many employees and, in this group, has all but destroyed confidence in the firm's leaders.

Because values, beliefs, and a sense of what is right are so vital to most people, wise leaders will very carefully consider actions or conditions that may violate important employee values. Whenever changes must be made that will significantly impact a company's core processes and structure, its people-focused systems, or its people themselves, I suggest that very serious thought be given to how key employees will evaluate the change. What will the impact be on employee self-confidence and self-respect of a change in the firm's strategic identity? One client executive has an informal group of employee advisors. They represent all levels and primary functions. Before making any change that may collide with core values, this leader asks, listens very carefully, and has sometimes dramatically modified the initial plan. She knows that core beliefs are drivers of how people feel about themselves. And she knows that healthy self-confidence is essential to sustained individual and company performance. For instance, leaders of a firm with a long and strong tradition of providing only top-quality products must be very careful not to violate that cultural value by demanding shipment of apparently shoddy merchandise.

Probably unknown to most consumers, a client of ours produces under two names essentially the same kind of product, but to entirely different levels of sophistication and quality. The top-quality brand has been the firm's mainstay for decades. The lower-quality product and name was acquired a few years ago.

The original intention was to greatly reduce costs by combining manufacturing of both products in a single facility. It didn't work because many people whose entire careers had been devoted to the top-quality brand resisted the "cheap" product at every step. It didn't fit the firm's identity or their own sense of what the company should be about. More than a few, including supervisors and managers, said that it was "wrong" to make something everyone knew was not very good. They found the whole idea to be morally offensive. Eventually, the company's leaders moved the second tier product to a different location and established a new corporation with its own, newly employed group of people to build the product.

Any perceived violation of a strongly held belief will degrade commitment. Conversely, even very difficult and stressful alterations can be well-received—if consistent with strong values.

> During the twenty-five years I've been here, whenever the company was in serious trouble the pay of all management people got temporarily cut the same percent. That hurt us first-level supervisors. We griped and moaned, but stayed on and did our very best because top management also took a hit, backed us up with the union, and never laid off a supervisor who performed well. Management has been fair with us.

This company's leaders must continue to put a high priority on upholding their end of this trade—highly valued support and transparently fair treatment for the critical first-level supervisors. In return, they can expect loyalty and full commitment from people whose self-respect is intact, despite enduring some tough situations.

The work environment where most of us spend so much of our lives is a maelstrom of intersecting, sometimes conflicting, values and beliefs. These beliefs are part of the unspoken, informal contract that most employees feel they have with their company and its leaders. Slogans and overblown executive value statements often do not fully reflect the real values held by the firm's people. Still less often do such pronouncements help guide action.

For instance, one textile company used to publish a widely derided policy. "Under no conditions will gifts or payments of any kind be paid to any entity that has an actual or potential commercial relationship with this company," and the statement went on to elaborate the theme. Sounds ethical and even pious. The problem was that the company has long done business in parts of the world where gifts, payments, and bribes are normal and expected practices used to speed approvals and actions. And nearly every one knew it.

Boards of directors that vote for, and executives who accept, extremely large pay increases while putting people out of work seriously degrade employee confidence and self-respect—and may ultimately damage the organization's ability to trade. We can both think of examples in electronics, finance, and airlines, to name just three. Such actions are usually evaluated by employees as morally and ethically wrong. It is only a matter of time before customers begin to experience the consequences. The self-interest of real leaders does not rely on such short-term, personal windfalls. It rests on successfully leading a company through turbulence to strength, to a sustained ability to satisfy customers, and to trade successfully.

In my experience, substantial organization change and redirection demands that leaders clearly, forcefully, and frequently articulate key values that largely resonate with what most employees already believe. Just *maintaining* a firm's existing strategic integrity is difficult when the business and regulatory environments are fluid. Under these conditions, too, people need reassurance that the driving values and beliefs are still reliable. Nucor's Ken Iverson is often interviewed by analysts and journalists. The values and beliefs he expresses are consistent, year by year. Nucor people and customers alike are reassured by such bedrock constancy. It is, in fact, rarely possible to rapidly introduce wholly new beliefs into a company. When attempted, confusion, disillusionment, and disbelief result. Individual and organization self-confidence decline, making the immediate problems even more difficult to resolve.

When Sears moved from its traditional top-quality, basic goods posture to stores comprised of stylish boutiques, the initial strategy failed because there was a major disconnect with the long-held values of both Sears' employees and its customers. Before initiating major change, leaders should devote the time necessary to understand and engage the organization's primary values as evaluated by all major constituencies.

For decades, many companies could be depended upon to be secure places to work. Perform to standard and you need have no concern about not having a job. That was a bold-letter provision in the informal contract between such firms and their people. It was a matter of faith and belief shared by hourly workers, managers, and top leaders alike.

Rapidly changing markets, competition, high costs, and poor company performance continue to require the leaders of many companies to close facilities, eliminate whole functions, and lay off hundreds of thousands of people. The traumatic financial consequences have been dramatic enough. Even more hurtful to those affected has been the perceived unilateral, top-down violation of the implied contract. From that perspective, *their* company and *their* leaders broke a binding promise. At an intellectual level, many dismissed people say they fully understand the reasons. At a visceral, emotional level there remain powerful feelings of betrayal, hurt, and anger. When core beliefs and values are violated, the damage to self-confidence will be enormous and often worse for those who survive than for those who do not.

However necessary such actions may have been, the violence done to self-assurance has been and will continue to be enormous. Probably only a few such companies will soon again enjoy the high stature, attractiveness, and employee commitment they once possessed. I suspect that the many abrupt passages from dependence on leaders and institutions to personal responsibility for one's self-respect will have profound corporate and generational consequences.

In a different way, we can only guess at the clash with ethical beliefs and resulting impact on commitment of the highly publicized price-fixing allegations at giant ADM. Archer Daniels Midland is a proud company with about $11 billion dollars of revenue and roughly 16,000 employees. Now, assertions of theft by one or more executives have also been added to the stew. I would be very surprised if all this is not the subject of much painful speculation in every plant and office. You can bet that customers and competitors aren't silent, either. Ethical and legal transgressions such as those alleged are counter to basic values and so have a corrosive effect on company image, employee self-confidence, and ultimately, performance. Such acts will also be emotionally evaluated as a major breach of the informal contract between every employee and the company's executive leaders.

Individual and company values do not operate in a vacuum. They will be expressed through and will sometimes alter selected strategies. Important beliefs and values can direct the way assets are used and also the output of organizations, people, and systems. Earlier, we saw how one company overwhelms just about everyone with huge, incredibly detailed reports. One result of such an expensive but unfocused system is to so cloud responsibility that no one feels responsible or can be held accountable. Detailed conversations with people at many levels convinced us that the leaders preferred to avoid and even deny conflict; they were strongly reluctant to confront failure or to demand results. A companywide employee survey elicited hundreds of anonymous, write-in comments. They specifically identified a widely held belief that top management vigorously denied existed:

> No one around here is really responsible for results.

> The midsized product was a total failure. No one could tell who to hold accountable.

> We tolerate repeated failures, and always have. We don't even know who did it. I don't think top management wants to know.

In this eighty-year-old company, it is clear that a long-held value for avoiding blame and numerous unfocused systems reinforce each other to the detriment of performance. Widely held belief systems, especially by leaders, can significantly alter the use and impact of the four change levers. They can also partially define the meaning of such characteristics as achievement. If avoiding blame and maintaining cordiality are valued, that's the way achievement will be assessed.

In one tightly focused missile system manufacturing operation, core values and achievement are highly congruent.

> We're about keeping any hostile missile from hitting anywhere in the U.S. . . . period. Never been a failure on launch. Never a failed intercept. Won't be—that's what counts. There's not one person here who won't stop everything if there's a problem.

The leaders of a company started about fifteen years ago recognized the linkages among the change levers and peoples' self-respect. The company produces highly specialized machine tools. The senior executives decided that a clear strategic identity would guide all important decisions:

1. Stay in or near our niche in the market. Stick close to what we know best and be the best at it.
2. Invest heavily in leading edge, but proven, technology. We are a manufacturer, not a research company.
3. Remain nonunion in an industry dominated by unions.
4. Be the most productive (profit per unit and sales per employee) in our industry, worldwide.

As a young company, they could and did carefully select highly achievement-oriented, financially motivated employees. An achievement-based incentive compensation system was devised that pays every employee handsomely for measured individual and unit performance. These executives knew that the kind of people they wanted to join the new company would not be attracted to a multilevel, power and influence dissipating hierarchy. So they have, to this day, only a relatively few levels. People in the separate facilities regularly make asset-use, personnel, and organization decisions reserved to corporate-level executives in competing firms.

The previous brief example shows the interplay of the primary management levers and several self-esteem components. When these connections are clear to everyone, the positive impact on trade will usually be considerable. Not coincidentally, under such conditions, leaders can concern themselves with larger, longer-range opportunities because the entire organization is largely self-managing.

Especially in larger organizations, top-level leaders cannot usually impact the firm's strategic identity or employee self-confidence directly or personally. Their realistic access is through the four architectural change levers. This is not to say that leaders should not take every opportunity to influence people face to face. They obviously should, and the best ones do. But as a practical matter, they must usually rely on other mechanisms, primarily the four levers and unremitting communication about the meaning of the firm.

The usual outcome from such a systemic leadership approach and tight linkages, is more trade. Drive the levers toward increased self-confidence for some years, and the organization's climate will change as a result, not a cause, of greater company effectiveness. The following statement was made by Dwight Byrd, president of Marion Composites, after approximately three or four years of just such a concentrated effort:

> It is a different place now. Much stronger, far more business, and lower costs. We're leaders. Morale is a lot higher, so is quality. It isn't the same company.

Interviews throughout the company confirm Byrd's assessment.

Persistent and sensitive movement of the four levers is an efficient way to engage peoples' desire for self-confidence and the only credible way to sharpen and define the firm's identity. When that happens, many elements of the culture will visibly change in some important ways. Long before that, though, trade will usually have increased. Like high pay, good jobs, and community assistance, positive culture change is a consequence of increased trade, not its cause.

One of the best ways for a leader to understand the organization's identity and real values is to ask customers about their personal experiences with the firm's people, products, and services. Confidential customer surveys and face-to-face executive contacts are good ways of finding out how the company's real values-in-use are perceived. Don't be surprised or discouraged when customer perceived values don't correspond to those proclaimed by leaders. Every lack of fit between the two is a major opportunity to improve.

When important employee values are openly supported by important leader behaviors, you can feel the pride and commitment. Rexnord Corporation made many industrial products. Among them were items that are used to attach jet engines to aircraft wings. Remember the tragic DC-10 crash in Chicago when an engine fell off? The directive of Rexnord's chairman and CEO was clear and unambiguous. *"Inspect the failed parts. See if they are ours. If they are, accept full responsibility at once. No hiding, no excuses."*

The failed bolts were *not* provided by Rexnord. But the chairman's response became part of a proudly recited tradition.

The owners of one company give every new employee a booklet that outlines how people are expected to act. I was especially impressed by one suggestion:

> During your career with us, you may be forced to make choices between what is right and what is easy or apparently profitable. Sometimes the choices won't be that clear. A good standard is to make the decision you wouldn't mind reading about on the front page of the newspaper. Do so and you'll never go very far wrong.

An adequate level of self-confidence is critical to both individual and company performance. To be sure, performance can, for a time, be maintained at a reasonable level even with low individual esteem and degraded firm identity, but a gradual decay is inevitable. Further, more and more time and energy must be applied to maintain the organization's performance in the face of low confidence and a progressively less positive company identity. That external energy sometimes takes the form of threats and pressure, or promises and implied potentials for future rewards. Like a partially plugged fuel line in your car, leaders have to push harder on the accelerator just to hold the same speed.

Companies with a crisp, affirmative identity and people whose self-respect is regularly renewed through their work require very much *less* external energy. Rather, they generate more of their own internal energy, freeing executive leaders for other activities. Leader behaviors that are consistent with primary beliefs and values add to employee self-confidence and to the organization's ability to trade successfully.

Last week a frustrated manager asked a question I've heard many times before:

> Look. With so much practical leadership experience around and thousands of research studies about leadership, what do we know for sure about leading organizations of people at work? Aren't there any universally applicable principles?

The short answers are: not very much and not very many. But there are a few, and they can be very powerful. I'm not sure how much agreement there would be, but here's my list.

1. There is a substantial body of dependable knowledge about how to select people who will probably perform very well. No leader can go wrong who directs that significant assets and systems be devoted toward selecting and engaging such people.
2. You will usually get the actions and outcomes you expect and, especially, measure. The more often you measure and post results for all to see, the more often you will get the expected outcomes. And if you measure, feed back results and PAY for what you want, you will almost surely get it. Be sure that what you measure and reward is really what you want.
3. Genuine participation works, especially if persistently supported by leaders who provide appropriate training, rewards, and personal commitment.

4. Giving people real power to decide important matters usually works even better than participation alone, if the right organization structure and a supportive climate are provided over an extended time.
5. If conditions are right, self-managed groups of people can achieve truly outstanding results.
6. Openness, honesty, and candor are almost always best; whether the issue is organization change, altered expectations, product or service performance, or a new competitive threat. Trust begets trust; so does mistrust. Only in a few specific circumstances (e.g., an acquisition) is it possible to communicate too much or too often.
7. Major short-term expedients that hurt people, though temporarily attractive, rarely yield satisfactory or predicted consequences. Exemplary success over time demands leaders with the will and courage to create, articulate, and visibly act in the service of a sustained system of beliefs—the organization's strategic identity. It is ultimately the responsibility of leaders to clearly define expectations.
8. Important changes, especially in an organization's culture, take substantially longer than leaders expect. Performance typically falls off before turning positive. Organization members need and deserve persistent and supportive leaders especially during such times of transition.

## SUMMARY

Alert outsiders who are not part of the company can usually see evidence of high employee self-confidence. Among the indicators I sometimes look for are:

- Few closed-door meetings or secretive huddles. Most transactions are open and free-flowing.
- There is a purposeful, but rarely harried or frenzied work climate.
- Many informal discussions and speculations among departments and levels.
- Many new ideas brought to the surface: lots of creative energy is evident. Even apparently wild ideas are listened to.

- Managers spend little energy searching for self-supportive information. Tasks, plans, problems, and solutions drive most interactions.
- Virtually no self-protective memos for file; no more paper than required.
- Great willingness to share opinions, facts, and feelings across organizational lines and hierarchy levels.
- Conflicts openly confronted in meetings; a fair amount of humor in meetings.
- Little reluctance to argue for one's opinion with those more senior in the hierarchy.
- Low, unplanned employee turnover.
- A minimal number of imposed controls.
- Standardized policies and procedures only where required for product integrity, safety, or other compelling reasons.
- Clarity and assurance about peoples' roles and functions.
- Little reluctance to bring problems to the surface; managers are rarely surprised.
- Little exaggeration of results or activities.
- Emphasis on results and outcomes, not on activity or looking busy. Most meetings are brief, brisk, and focused.
- Emphasis on personal or knowledge power rather than position power or rank.

When you see a preponderance of these kinds of indicators, you can bet that most people feel self-confident and assured. In such firms, I usually find that just about anyone you ask can define and describe what the place really is—its purpose and identity.

Reverse these observations, and you probably have a troubled company and people with a low sense of self-respect and value. Without clear and energetic action by the firm's leaders, its products and services are likely to falter, and customer satisfaction will likely decline.

Many times, the basic approach to directing a company with a fuzzy or weak identity and people with low self-confidence is defensive and reactive. Leadership of an organization with a crisp, strong identity and self-assured people tends to be more proactive, optimistic, and opportunity-oriented. These characteristic ways of acting tend to hold true whether basic business conditions are good or bad. The critical factors are the organization's strategic identity and the self-esteem of its members.

The most effective leaders I know focus continuously and carefully on improving the effective use of the four architectural components. They recognize that such alterations are, for the most part, almost immediately visible embodiments of their plans, values, and expectations. Changes in any or all of the four are both substantive and symbolic of top-management intentions. And they are always the subjects of intense discussion far beyond the executive suite. Very few officially sanctioned, corporate communications will elicit half so much interest or send so crisp a message.

Effective leaders also pay at least equal attention to maintaining and even enhancing employee confidence, commitment, and self-esteem, especially during times of stress and change. They know that the organization's long-term ability to satisfy customers cannot be enhanced by changing the architecture while the foundations are permitted to crumble. These executives typically institute policies and practices that are expected to lift employee self-esteem, to demonstrate unequivocally that people are genuinely valued, contributing colleagues in the business of increasing trade.

Leaders who ignore emotions and pursue change only through exhortation and a top-down, unfeeling manipulation of the architectural components, will usually achieve only short-lived success, often at the cost of the organization's ability to trade successfully in the future. Even if temporarily successful, such a tactic usually fails. Those who pay are the firm's people and owners. Unfortunately, many shortsighted leaders manage to maintain and even enhance their own financial status, if not their reputations.

# SECTION IV: CUSTOMERS— THE POINT OF IT ALL

FIGURE 7. The Role of Customer Satisfaction in Trade

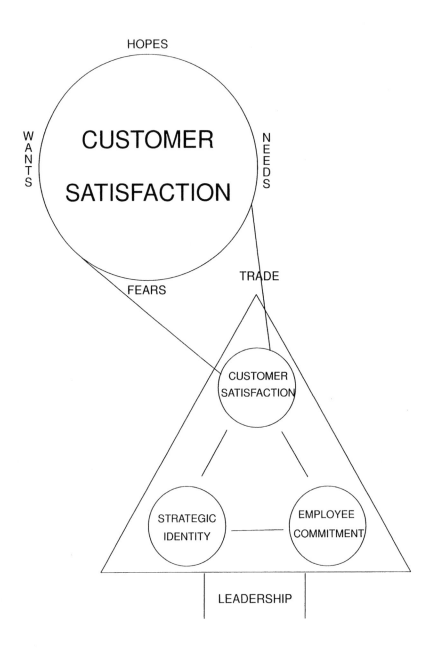

*Every man takes the limits of his own field of vision for the limits of the world.*

—Shopenhauer

The sole purpose of any product or service provider is to engage in trade. Any exchange requires someone or some other entity to trade with—a customer. Whether called a client, patient, customer, or trading partner, the purpose of the relationship is the same—an exchange.

The only guarantors of continuing trade are people who are willing to exchange something of value with you. They will only do so if they expect to be satisfied. Over the longer term, it takes the actions of skilled, self-assured, and committed people to meet the wants and needs of others. This and the allocation of assets are usually the twin engines of most successful leadership initiatives. In recent years, a number of excellent books have been published that provide explicit techniques to satisfy customers in a range of different industries. My purpose here is not to repeat those helpful admonitions but, rather, to provide a framework for thinking about primary customer characteristics and for linking them to the firm's identity and to its people.

Fortunately, customers are not mysterious. What counts with our customers is also important to each of us, simply because each one of us has long been a customer for all kinds of goods and services. We already know what tends to attract us to a particular vendor and what it takes to satisfy. But, you may say, "That's all different when both the seller and buyer are big companies." Certainly, some conditions are different, but the basics are the same.

Ultimately, companies don't buy or sell, people do. Yes, the contract or the check may bear the name of a remote purchasing manager or controller. But most times, someone else invited you to make a proposal and decided whether or not to buy. Trading of any kind is an exploration; it is a clarifying and decision process among people. It is not usually a remote or mechanical procedure between institutions. And that is convenient because it means that we already know a lot about what will satisfy customers—the same things that will satisfy us as individuals.

Four primary concerns are involved in any significant purchase. Meeting them will in large measure determine whether we elect to trade with the same individual or entity again. They define for customers their level of satisfaction. As I have observed it, the same concerns exist regardless of what is bought, so long as the goods or services are truly important to the acquirer.

Usually some *need* or group of needs are the reasons someone decides to act, by developing specifications, seeking funds and vendors, and issuing purchase orders or contracts, for examples.

A *need* is fairly pressing and, in some form, is a necessity. For instance, with 200,000 miles on the odometer, a newer car of some kind is likely to be a need. Here are some concerns any customer might have:

- Is what I need available in the market now or soon?
- Will the price be what I/we are willing to pay?
- Can I/we depend on it to perform as expected?
- Will it "work" sufficiently well to satisfy everyone; i.e., my wife, my boss, or the vice president?
- Can I count on it to be delivered when agreed?
- Will the seller truly make good anything not satisfactory?

In addition to fairly immediate needs there are *wants,* which exceed the need in some way. Wants go beyond the minimum requirements of the RFP or request for proposal. Wants are nice-to-have or useful characteristics and features hoped for, perhaps, but not really expected. Most of us don't expect to receive superb personal service very often. If it happens, we will be surprised and delighted. When thinking about wants, issues such as these arise:

- Is this product/service/vendor likely to deliver even more than contracted or expected?
- Will it make important others happy with me and be more than just acceptable?
- Can this product or seller meet our future as well as present needs?
- Is this vendor likely to continuously improve quality, design, delivery, and price?

- If future transactions are likely, can I expect a relationship with this vendor to become one of trust, honesty, and predictability?

Along with wants and needs, every purchaser of a major product or service *hopes* for a predictable, pleasant, painless experience. In the corporate world, one frequent and fervent hope is that the acquisition will satisfy everyone in power and avoid any personal censure for a poor decision. Which is one reason that so many company buying decisions are referred to one or even several committees.

A primary *hope* for all of us is that in retrospect the expenditure proves to have been sound to everyone concerned.

- We hope it all works out as we and important others wish.
- We hope there are no unpleasant surprises.
- We hope the purveyor becomes a true partner and source of dependable interest and continuing help.

And, of course, there is also the reversal of hope—*fear.* Anytime there is much at stake, there is likely to be some anxiety and concern, perhaps even fear.

Will the new model sell or is it another Edsel?
Can I successfully run the company we just bought?
Do I dare go to the board for money for the new product?

Or at a more personal level:

Is this the best surgeon I can find?
Can I handle the mortgage payments
Will I have the assets for the kids' education?

All of these are examples of major trades that carry with them uncertainty and questions such as:

- Can I do it? Should I? Dare I?
- Will it satisfy everyone?
- Will it truly be as expected in all respects?
- Is the seller really experienced, competent, and trustworthy?
- What can I do if "it" doesn't work out?

Anytime an important deal is pending or recently concluded, you can expect that these four kinds of issues will occupy a major share-of-attention of anyone who has much at stake.

When fears and hopes, wants and needs are effectively controlled and managed, most customers will be well satisfied with both the provider and the transaction; they will strongly tend to buy again from the same source.

A lot of conditions and circumstances will determine whether a business or professional firm succeeds over the years. Leaders can, in fact, control or even substantially influence many fewer of these determining conditions than their people and most outsiders usually believe.

What leaders *can* do is to largely determine how the four architectural levers will be engaged to define, continually refine, and energize the firm's strategic identity. Leaders can use those same factors to enable and encourage the growth of healthy levels of self-respect and self-confidence. And leaders are ultimately responsible for satisfying customers.

# Chapter 13

# Customer Needs and Wants

Generations of managers and executives have been exposed to a variety of useful motivational models and techniques. Considerable research has confirmed the importance of individual needs to human behavior. We know that satisfying some basic needs leads to employee commitment and satisfaction. From Theory Y to the Hierarchy of Needs, from Motivation-Hygiene to Expectancy and Esteem Theory, much is known about the motivations and consequent actions of people at work.

In more recent years, many attempts have been made to expand some of these motivation models, to explicitly categorize and measure consumer needs, and to predict behavior. Various population characteristics and components of social and economic standing have been similarly employed in efforts to explain consumer needs and subsequent behaviors. These demo- and psychographic models have been tantalizing but only moderately successful so far.

I suggest that we begin with Carl Sewell's dictum: "Find out what the customer *wants* and give it to him." (emphasis added)

Sewell has one part of the equation exactly right. But as we have seen, wants are only one of four customer concerns. To better understand your customers, ask and listen very carefully. For instance, you might use questionnaires at the point of purchase, to accompany the service or product, or to be transmitted later. Customer focus groups can also be helpful in suggesting new avenues to explore. But a genuinely interested face-to-face inquiry is usually best when practical. A retailer may have to depend on carefully constructed questionnaires and sales numbers while the executives of a machine tool manufacturer may be able to personally visit every customer. The physically closer you can get to your customer, the better. Sometimes questionnaires and surveys can be combined with face-to-face conversations, video conferencing, or telephone contact with very positive results. But the research must be designed and performed competently by trained people. With that caveat, customer views can be important to the leaders of almost any kind of firm.

A law firm surveyed its corporate clients by mail. The results clearly showed that the firm's smaller corporate customers were well satisfied while the leaders of its very large clients were decidedly not. Face-to-face meetings showed that the smaller customers usually purchased advice and counsel about clearly defined problems. Their needs and their assignments were specific and limited.

At the same time, executives in many of the firm's large corporate customers tended to off-load a large number and variety of often ill-defined problems to the outside law firm. The invoice amounts were huge and the source of considerable unhappiness. Face-to-face meetings between several of the firm's partners and client executives rebuilt the quality of the endangered relationship. While billings to the largest customers have declined their satisfaction is now much higher; so is the likelihood of conti^ued, profitable assignments.

Finding out what the customer needs and wants isn't always easy, but it is almost certain to be worth the effort if the investigation explores matters beyond just the singular service or product provided. Remember, you want customers who are satisfied with *every* point of contact with your company.

A software development client asked us to find out how satisfied their business customers were with the performance of the very sophisticated software systems our client provided. We persuaded them to allow us to inquire about other aspects of the relationship beyond just system performance. The results were somewhat surprising. Almost without question, customers said that the systems usually performed exceedingly well, just as promised, and that the prices charged were, on balance, competitive if not reasonable. What drove customer executives crazy were delivery promises that were almost never met, coupled with no credible effort to provide an explanation for the delays. Nothing was done on time, and no one seemed to know why. The dress and demeanor of some of the software provider's on-site staff were also offensive to some senior members of their old-line investment firm clients. These problems have been largely corrected as shown by repeat surveys and, most important, by face-to-face meetings. To find out what your customers need and want, ask in as many ways as you can. Be sure that any survey's introduction, design, sample, and analysis are transparently objective and professional.

Wants and needs may not be the same thing; the two are sometimes confused. I may *need* transportation but *want* a Corvette that I may not be able to afford. When I visit the Chevrolet dealership, economics may tend to force my needs and wants to be more nearly the same. One job of a salesman is to meet my immediate *need* and at the same time move me toward meeting my *want,* perhaps with a new financing or leasing approach for a nicer car.

Needs tend to be more immediate than wants. A customer may need an accounting software package that can be operational in days or weeks, but may want a wholly redesigned process and a much more embracing type of hardware and software system. Meeting customer needs often tends to require relatively short-term solutions, while fulfilling wants often calls for rethinking and reconfiguring entire structures, products, and processes.

Understanding customer needs is often fairly easy, while determining and meeting customer wants usually demands deeper study and appreciation of the customer's future intentions and likely environment. Ideally, customer wants and needs will be parallel tracks or at least not in conflict. Sometimes, though, the two are in opposition.

We once had a financially troubled textile client. Some of the firm's leaders were absolutely determined to thwart a strongly supported union-organizing effort regardless of means or costs required. The show-of-interest cards showed over 70 percent support for the union. At the same time, our research clearly showed that increased employee productivity and commitment would be essential to financial recovery. We strongly advised our client to avoid "union-busting" actions that might result in lasting employee hostility. Instead, we urged steps to regain employee confidence and loyalty with or without a union. In this case, some wants and needs were opposed. Fortunately, intercession by top-level executives brought the two much closer together. The employees did vote for a union but in a calm atmosphere without excessive threats and bombast. Today, company-employee relations are sound and productive.

Surveys, focus groups, one-to-one conversations, and other techniques can be effective for discovering what customers need, right now, from your product or service offerings. But such methodologies can do much more. They can inform about customer wants and future intentions. They can also show unexpected ways you can provide real value to your customers beyond your primary service or product.

One well-known equipment manufacturer discovered that while its products were very highly evaluated by its industrial customers, its invoicing procedure was not. Our survey had deliberately and specifically probed every area of contact between the provider and its customers—quality, delivery, billing, design, marketing, etc. Customer executives were almost unanimous: "Your products are great, but we've never been able to integrate your invoicing into our system without a lot of work." Easy to fix, easy to add real and appreciated value to the customer, easy to satisfy both needs and wants.

Discovering and anticipating the true wants of a business customer usually involves much more than studying an RFQ (request for quotation), talking to a buyer, or schmoozing with a contracts manager, though all three may be important activities. For instance, custom designed, high-speed equipment makers have told me that it isn't unusual for a customer's quality assurance executive to insist that the equipment have many possible adjustments so that very tight tolerances can be maintained. At the same time, manufacturing executives in the same firm want equipment that will operate at high speeds with little attention and minimal need to train operators or maintenance technicians.

This example highlights two issues. First, customer desires are often not the same among different customers or even within a single customer entity. Second, needs and wants are not necessarily the same. Reconciling these differences should involve nearly every major business function in the providing firm—not just sales or marketing.

Customer *needs* can usually be determined, if not always accommodated, with reasonable accuracy. Understanding business customer *wants* is often more difficult; it requires an awareness of the business customer's objectives, plans, and ultimate customers. For instance, many electronic cameras, laptop computers, toys, and other devices have cavities for batteries. Often these "holes" are rectangular in shape because of the geometry of the other critical components, such as circuit boards. Yet some battery makers make only cylinder-shaped cells for the equipment. Clearly, there is unused space when a cylinder is fitted into a rectangular hole. That wasted space could be used perhaps for larger, more powerful batteries that could enhance the performance of the existing product and customer satisfaction along with it. More or longer-lasting battery power might permit equipment designers to add new or desired features thereby increasing sales, profitability, or both. It requires investment, but learning all you can about what customers need— and what they really want—is an important way to focus the organization and to improve trade.

A company we work with provides very sophisticated and expensive components to the aerospace industry. The technical people who design and build such apparatus know their customers' needs and wants. They understand the customers' systems, people, and organizations and they know a great deal about the ultimate customer, the Department of Defense.

Now, in the defense business the usual pattern is for an RFP (request for proposal) to be issued and for a number of suppliers to respond with very detailed proposals that meet all technical, delivery, and performance requirements contained in the RFP. Frequently, several bids meet all specifications and differ only on price. A lot of contracts are won with prices so low that there's little or no profit, only some overhead absorption.

Our client's strategy is to respond to such RFPs in the usual way with a proposal that meets the customer's needs. But they also submit a parallel response, one that addresses other matters that they believe are among their customer's wants. So, they offer a higher-priced alternative design that promises added benefits and advantages. Over half of the time, customers select the higher-priced offering that meets both needs and wants.

Cities and other governmental bodies have begun to examine citizen wants and needs separately. Surveys, informal contacts, and the persuasive pleas of various advocacy groups show elected leaders pretty clearly what services are wanted. More sophisticated decision methodologies that take account of service costs and perceived effectiveness are being used to more crisply define real needs separately from wants. Under conditions of constrained resources, distinguishing between wants and needs has become critically important to governments, as it has always been for most businesses and individuals.

To provide offerings that meet both the needs and wants of customers demands the allocation of assets and, equally, the focused actions of skilled and committed people. Intentions to provide exemplary, value adding offerings must be supported by appropriate systems. People must be selected, trained, equipped, informed, assisted, and compensated in ways that promote actions that will lead to customer satisfaction. Organization structures, roles, and processes should be regularly examined and adjusted for contribution. All this is far more than simple downsizing or redesigning business processes, though both may be necessary. Achieving long-term customer satisfaction demands committed, competent people empowered to achieve in a great many ways and who are visibly valued and recognized for their contributions. When these conditions exist, the real meaning of the company will be clear to all, and its customers are very likely to be satisfied.

# Chapter 14

# Hopes and Fears

Every potential and actual customer, client, patient, and trading partner *hopes* for something from the relationship. Usually there is an array of expectations ranging from fervent hope to utter cynicism, from wildly unrealistic to thoroughly objective, from fuzzy to clear. Such hopes often determine whether the trading relationship will begin in the first place and significantly impact whether it will be satisfying and endure. Wants and hopes are not the same. In my experience an unmet customer hope is the single most important source of lawsuits, failures to pay, and dissatisfaction with product or service. Flawed services and products are certainly the most obvious causes of unmet customer needs. Systems and strategies such as TQM, ISO certification, peer review, process redesign, and their functional equivalents have helped many companies to improve the quality of their offerings significantly. Achieving and maintaining demonstrably high levels of quality and performance must be high on any customer-focused priority list.

But, a product or service may fully meet or even exceed professional, industry, or specification requirements, and all customary standards and still fail to fulfill a customer's hopes. The main reasons are:

- Overblown claims and promises by the provider
- Misunderstanding about what the customer really wants—a shared responsibility
- Unrealistic, uncommunicated, and often emotionally based hopes of the purchaser

My endodontist provides every patient with detailed drawings of what a particular procedure will entail. In bold print is a statement to the effect that although the procedure is 90 to 95 percent effective, it deals with organic materials and, therefore, cannot be guaranteed. More important, time is devoted to discussing with each patient the steps to be taken, likely outcomes, and what the patient can anticipate. From the patient, this practitioner solicits very detailed symptomology, previous health problems, and choices about treatment. It is an attempt to establish altogether clear, mutually acceptable expectations. The need for treatment is obvious, but wants, fears, and, especially, hopes may not be clear without considerable interchange and exploration. Hopes and fears are usually emotional. An executive may engage a household name firm to analyze data even though he knows that others can provide even better service at less cost. He engages the better-known vendor to avoid the fear of risk and blame from his superiors if the result fails to meet their expectations. "You can't blame me; I hired Smith and Company."

A person-to-person process of defining hopes can only be approximated by large-volume providers through techniques such as surveys, literature, demonstrations, product tests, interviews, and focus groups. But every reasonable effort should be made to assure clarity of key customer hopes and fears. In advertisements and other product or service descriptions more care than is often the case should be taken to avoid establishing or enhancing any unwarranted hopes by purchasers. The difference between aggressive marketing and establishing unrealistic expectations is often not clear. It is an area that calls for careful thought, testing, and decision before the fact.

Despite all best efforts to be clear and honest, some few purchasers will still hold to unstated and even mutually conflicting hopes about the product or service. An owner of a small company, who also handled most sales activities, once asked us to perform a study and recommend an organization structure that would facilitate growth. That was the clearly stated need. The study was well-designed and conscientiously carried out. The conclusions and recommendations were well supported and, I believe, sound. But the client was totally dissatisfied because he hoped for a recommended structure that would allow him to be away from the business several days each week. Any such structure would have been completely unrealistic given the assets and demands of the business. It would also have conflicted with the stated growth objective. These restraints made no difference to him. We met the need; clearly we did not meet his hopes. As in this case, hopes and expectations are often unacknowledged, emotional, and sometimes in direct conflict with conscious needs. It isn't always possible to know this in advance, but when it is, I recommend withdrawing from the potential transaction. No sale is worth the likely outcome of a dissatisfied customer. Not all trade is good business.

The speed of change and simple passage of time can also cause purchaser hopes and provider intentions to diverge. I once owned one of the more expensive Japanese-made cars. It stranded me—after 65,000 miles—one night when something called a serpentine timing belt apparently broke. I felt cheated by the manufacturer and by the dealer. The last time I looked into a car's engine, a long time ago, there was a rugged timing chain, not a belt. I was unaware that there *was* a belt or that it should be routinely replaced. Technology had moved well ahead of my knowledge. A wise dealer might have avoided the problem with some timely information near the time of recommended replacement.

The point is that when I bought the car someone may have mentioned the eventual need to replace the belt. But the warning could have been repeated several years later when "eventual" was becoming "soon." To avoid violating customer hopes, be sure to keep the communication channels open well after the sale of your goods or services. Find out if what was purchased is still satisfactory. Pass along any useful tips or suggestions. Such practices can avoid disrupted customer expectations and may even result in more trade.

When customer needs and wants are reasonably congruent, and when hopes are realistic and clear to all parties, customer satisfaction is a likely result provided, of course, that the products and services perform properly.

Achieving clear, mutually agreed expectations is fundamentally a person-to-person process. It cannot usually be delegated to lawyers, nor can hopes and fears be easily reduced to unambiguous contract language because they are fundamentally feelings. Certainly, many agreements may need to be formalized, but the face-to-face process of negotiating shared hopes and expectations is often vital. Regular review and renegotiation as the relationship proceeds is a key to satisfaction and long-term trade.

A large shipper once told me that no more than 20 to 25 percent of his delivery agreements were written into a formal document. Something like that proportion is true for our twenty-five-year-old management advisory firm as well. Both of us prefer to work intensively, face to face, with actual and potential customers. A written contract, if there is one, is usually a mechanical, pro forma document or a letter of understanding.

Large organizations rarely speak with one voice. Nor are customer people always sure about what they want, need, or hope for from a service or product provider. Moreover, a senior executive's evaluation of a service or product is likely to be highly influenced by what he or she is told by lower-positioned people. If the task is large or complex, I sometimes recommend a team approach to defining customer-leader wants, needs, hopes, and fears before undertaking the project. If at all practical, you might create a "discovery team" of people representing a variety of skills, levels, and functions. Their task is not merely to observe but to actively seek out wants, needs, fears, and hopes from customer experts and opinion leaders at multiple levels. The more nearly your offering can be tailored to match the constellation of customer desires, the more likely is satisfaction and future trade.

We have clients who have carefully selected and trained people who can be quickly formed into ad hoc, customer-focused teams. Their purpose is not to sell or market anything. Their goal is to help define and clarify customer expectations and concerns. They are especially alert to any worries, concerns, and fears that can be addressed in future presentations and proposals. For the same purpose, in our firm we want to meet with several senior-level leaders before undertaking any significant assignment. When we haven't, it has usually been a mistake.

Knowing what actual or potential customers want, what they may need, and what is truly hoped for from your offering is not a matter of marketing intuition or black magic. It demands the deployment of assets. Systems, organization processes, and staffing actions have to be focused for that purpose.

Testing, delivering, and continuously modifying your offerings against customer desires demands employee skills and commitment of a high order. Only employees who enjoy a respectable level of self-confidence from work are interested or capable of providing the intense, creative, and persistent effort required.

# Chapter 15

# Benefits and Added Value

Marketing and sales executives are expected to focus on showing how customers will benefit from their firm's offered products and services. That's supposed to be their job. People in manufacturing are supposed to make things. Engineering folks are assigned to design them, and so on. We're all supposed to stay in our assigned organization boxes. That is no way to provide maximum value to customers or to enhance the growth and development of people.

## *INVOLVE EVERYONE IN PROVIDING BENEFITS*

Many, perhaps even most, primary business functions and departments can add noticed and appreciated value to customers well beyond the specific service or product offered. In many companies, flatter organization structures have helped to break down historic, functional hierarchies and vertical organization chimneys—a type of organization that tends to limit peoples' contribution to a particular function or specialty. More frequently now, employees in manufacturing are vigorously helping people in marketing. Finance experts are working on the shop floor with manufacturing specialists and with their counterparts in customer organizations. HR people are busy devising true, incentive compensation systems and actively involving union employees in product design, shop layout and cycle time reduction, to name just three. It is a far more fluid and, yes, more anxiety-producing situation than that of twenty years ago. Much of the focus of such activities is on improving internal effectiveness through lower costs, better quality, and faster response, all of which are also very helpful to customers. In some firms, added value to customers is being provided by representatives of many functional specialties and departments, such as accounting, data processing, and engineering. Every point of contact between provider and customer has the potential for increasing your value. The more mutually beneficial a relationship, the more likely is long-term trade. It is almost always less costly to retain existing customers than to attract new ones.

### LEARN WHAT WILL REALLY ADD VALUE

It is a powerful strategy to provide more value to your customer than expected or than your competitor does. But first, you need to know what extra benefits will be noticed and valued.

If you and your competitor sell essentially the same thing, what extra can you provide that will be clearly evaluated as an extra benefit? What characteristics or features can be added to your primary offerings, whether things or services, that customers will value and want?

For years, sailboat manufacturers went to considerable cost and effort to design interiors that were supposed to accommodate an outlandishly large number of people. So, the makers designed all kinds of creative folding, lowering, and pull-out platforms for eating and sleeping, say, six adults in a twenty-five-foot hull. Well, maybe, if they were very small, very friendly, and didn't mind crawling over each other to get out. The point is, such characteristics were rarely felt to be benefits by experienced sailors who knew they would never have that many people aboard for more than an afternoon. In recent years, many boat manufacturers have developed far more practical layouts, largely as a result of asking sailors what they wanted and by testing prototypes in actual use.

Tire makers advertise consumer tires they say are designed to run 140 miles an hour. Why? I doubt many of us see that as adding much value. A medical clinic advertises its wonderful (and certainly expensive) multistory atrium waiting area as a benefit. I suppose that is a nice touch, but reducing waiting time would probably be seen by most patients to be a much greater benefit.

Characteristics you think are benefits may not be considered benefits by your customer. Before introducing expensive changes, test whether they will be perceived to be genuine benefits. Will the changes better meet customer wants, reduce concerns, or satisfy hopes? Invite customers to examine prototypes. Create expert panels of users to suggest and evaluate. Survey samples of existing owner-users. It is easy to become so committed to the novel, creative, and different that we neglect to find out what the true value is from the customer's perspective.

## ADVERTISE THE VALUE YOU ADD

Even very desirable product or service characteristics may not be valued if customers don't know about them. Some auto companies and some dealerships have done an excellent job in promising purchasers:

> If you break down, for any reason, we will help you. Any time, any place.

To me, that's a real benefit of doing business with such a dealership. But many providers have not developed, or at least don't describe, any special benefit of trading with them. Our law firm can and does provide advice and legal help to our frequently traveling consultants at unusual times and places, and has for over two decades. But they don't tell anyone about their exceptional level of service. It doesn't happen very often, but it is an appreciated service. I wonder if a modest marketing effort directed to selected professional and other firms might bring new clients?

Mercury Marine goes to extraordinary lengths to make sure every single engine operates dependably and reliably before it leaves the factory. Yet their literature stresses technology and performance factors such as power, speed, and acceleration. I suspect that many boaters put a lot higher value on the absolute dependability Mercury works so hard to provide but doesn't talk about very much.

There are many individuals and companies who have provided us with extraordinary products and services over the years. You can probably make a similar list. Most seem to think that what they do so well should be the norm. It should be, but it isn't. If your offerings or your firm provide unusual value, say so. There's no reason to be reticent about important parts of the company's identity that help to satisfy its customers.

## *VALUE VERSUS BENEFIT*

Benefits are what you try to sell, and what you think you provide. Value is what your customers hope to receive. A long-term trading relationship usually requires that the two are at least equal or, if not, that value be the greater. Products and services that meet customer needs, add perceived value, and do not disappoint hopes will result in high levels of customer satisfaction and increased trade.

A national software provider found that their products got high marks. But their business customers greatly missed the personal knowledge and close contact with field representatives when the field service function was suddenly centralized in one city. It was expensive to fix this problem that could easily have been anticipated and avoided by asking and listening before making the change. The field people provided much more perceived value than corporate officials suspected.

While discovering what your customers want and need from your products or services, don't neglect to find out what value can be added to their other contacts and transactions with you. Adding value in these areas can also add to overall satisfaction and to the likelihood of future business.

# Chapter 16

# Satisfaction and a Word About Suppliers

A customer's level of satisfaction is the summary of feelings and evaluations about needs and wants, hopes and fears. Suppliers who meet these concerns will be seen as those that add significant value. Satisfaction is not a simple or unitary outcome. It is, though, a single index that can tell us how we are doing right now and whether or not our efforts are measurably succeeding. Some might argue that the real measures of satisfaction are financial, such as volume and margin changes. True enough, as far as it goes.

One problem with purely financial measures is that they tend to lag behind, sometimes by years, changes in customer satisfaction that will probably influence buying decisions well into the future. Low levels of customer satisfaction with the quality of U.S.-built automobiles in the early 1980s resulted in loss of market share to Japanese makers even years later when the quality differences had effectively disappeared. People long remember being dissatisfied with a major trade. I once owned two successive electric drills from the same well-known manufacturer. Both literally disintegrated in use. Irrationally, perhaps, I determined to never again buy such tools from that maker, even though the tools were probably not designed for the demanding tasks I required of them. Zebco (fishing rods and reels of many kinds) invested heavily for many years to overcome its once "cheap and shoddy" reputation and low customer satisfaction. When compared with the best equipment on the market today, Zebco products are fully competitive, and measured customer satisfaction is high. The company is also very profitable. I have been told that Zebco's improved designs, better materials, and much higher-quality reels were in the market well before customer satisfaction indicators similarly improved. Even after that, several years were required before the company achieved its volume and margin targets.

There is a second difficulty with relying solely on financial indicators. Not only do such indicators typically lag behind changes in customer perceptions, but they may temporarily change independently of such perceptions. And, of course, a change in the sales numbers does not explain *why* the change occurred.

In my observation, the most common causes of volume and margin improvements, that are largely unrelated to customer perceptions, are price and supply. The massive restructuring of the U.S. defense industry, for instance, has resulted in many fewer suppliers for some kinds of products. As a consequence, procurement officers sometimes buy less desired products simply because there are no other vendors, or at least no other bidders. Purchasing people in many industries have often been forced to accept less valued products for the same reason. It is a time of great shifting and uncertainty in many commercial relationships. Sometimes these shifts can temporarily work to improve an organization's sales volume or margins even though its offerings are low rated. If you don't test and measure customer perceptions, you might assume higher levels of satisfaction than really exist. While comforting, such an untested assumption can prove devastating when new alternatives and new competitors appear or when you attempt to introduce new offerings in the future.

If a product or service is priced low enough, many may buy it even though their past experience with the provider was not satisfactory, and their hopes are minimal. Priced low enough, I might buy another drill from the same manufacturer. It would have to be *much* cheaper than alternatives. This is a dangerous strategy, that of substituting low price for real customer satisfaction. Remember the Yugo car? Eventually, trade will likely vanish and so will your profits. Someone can usually make it cheaper and sell it for even less if there is a large enough market.

There is no adequate substitute for understanding how well you are meeting your customers' needs, wants, and hopes, summed up as their satisfaction, with your services and products. In automobile manufacturing, an increase of just one percentage point in customer loyalty has been estimated by *Automotive News* to be worth upward of $100 million in profits. Although the car companies, and the best of their dealers, have been leaders in measuring customer satisfaction, there's no reason to suppose that customer satisfaction is less important in any other business.

In previous chapters several methodologies for assessing customer views have been briefly mentioned. Of those, the following seem to be the most commonly used:

- Surveys of customer-leaders and other customer people and end users who purchase and use your products or services and, perhaps, those of competitors.
- Ad hoc and other kinds of focus groups of customers or customer representatives.
- Individual interviews with users or samples of users, by phone or in person.
- Visits to business customer locations by multilevel, multifunctional teams who observe your products in use and discuss them with their counterparts.

The term "survey" is a general one, with many meanings. Whether seeking to measure either customer *or* employee perceptions, one key distinction is between diagnostic and normative types of surveys. While the two may sometimes look much alike, the purposes are basically different.

*Normative* surveys are largely intended, designed, and analyzed to provide comparisons among the products, practices, and services of different providers. For instance, firms, such as J. D. Power, Inc., regularly measure customer satisfaction with many brands of cars. Every customer gets the same questions and every brand is evaluated in the same way against the same questions. From these data, they calculate an index and ranking for each brand against all the others. The outcome of a normative survey can tell you quite accurately how you compare, overall, with your competition; but in its purest form, a normative survey cannot tell you specifically why you scored well or how to get better. That is also true about normative employee attitude and opinion surveys. You may learn, for instance, that your people are much more satisfied with their supervision than employees in general. That's certainly gratifying and reason to celebrate. But it doesn't show what, exactly, your supervisors are doing differently. Such information would be very helpful in supervisory selection and training efforts, for instance.

There are firms that specialize in employee attitude surveys. Most of them have largely standard categories, scales, and questions designed to compare one group of employees' opinions with those of employees from many other companies. For instance, people in a particular company might be shown to be an average of 10 percent less satisfied with their benefits than are 50,000 previously surveyed people in twelve similar organizations. That is certainly worth knowing, must as it may be to know that Lexus cars have a higher customer satisfaction score than do Chevrolets. But neither result shows how important a finding is or what to do about it. After all, if a Lexus is far too expensive for you to consider, its customer satisfaction score may be of only very modest interest.

*Diagnostic* surveys are custom designed to measure customer or employee views, usually after considerable front-end study. They are developed and analyzed to focus on conditions and situations unique to a particular product or business organization. The intent is to discover exactly what people like or dislike about working at *this* particular company or driving *that* specific car. The purpose is to find out very specifically where and how to make improvement,; not to provide comparisons with other companies or products.

A typical diagnostic survey is grounded on conditions unique to the particular purpose. For instance, a diagnostic customer-satisfaction survey will usually ask for detailed suggestions and problem descriptions. It will also include quantitative items that indicate how important or widespread a specific issue is.

*Normative* surveys are useful when you want overall comparisons or if the number of respondents is very large. Such surveys can be fairly brief and are easily scored and analyzed. *Diagnostic* surveys are most effective when you want a tight focus, detailed views, and improvement suggestions. Diagnostic surveys require more preparation and analysis. They are more expensive, especially when the number of respondents is very large.

Some characteristics of diagnostic and normative surveys can, technically, be combined, and there are ways of controlling costs. The point is that there are various survey methodologies available, depending on purpose and other factors. Surveys are a very effective way of finding out what your customers, your employees, and even suppliers need, want, and actually experience from being associated with your company.

Another technique, the focus group, has moved from its early use in advertising to applications in such areas as product and service design, psychographics, politics, and assessing customer satisfaction. As with surveys, there are specialists in conducting focus group studies. By their nature, focus groups are not nearly so quantitative as surveys nor are they as amenable to statistical analysis and projection. Focus groups, like surveys and individual interviews, require specialized training and experience to be most useful. On balance, focus groups seem most helpful when you need a broad range of individual ideas, experiences, and expressions, and when a small number of respondents is adequate. By its basic design, focus group research gets expensive when large numbers of people are involved. Cost considerations usually mean that only a few customers or employees can be involved. In some situations, such as an exploratory study or with a small number of customers, such procedures can be very useful.

Whatever the methodology chosen, I suggest that few efforts are more important than discovering how satisfied your customers, suppliers, and employees are, and how they think you can improve.

## SUPPLIERS

The determination of skilled, confident people and the allocation of resources are required to fully satisfy customers. It should be a matter of highest strategic importance.

For many companies it is equally important to *be* a good customer. The quality of relationships with your suppliers and vendors can have dramatic impact on your ability to satisfy your own customers. A 1995 newspaper article demonstrated this point.

It seems that a major car maker had, by reason of its immense importance, steadily driven down the price it would pay for engine manifolds purchased from a relatively tiny supplier. Manifolds are designed to fit specific engines, and there is a limited market for such products, though there are a number of providers. Presumably, the supplier executives felt they had little choice but to accept the price offered by what must have been a hugely dominant customer.

The problem arose when the supplier's production equipment failed, and it was unable to produce and ship manifolds to its customer. The dictated low price had prevented the supplier from acquiring backup machinery. As a consequence, the automaker could not ship completed cars to its very unhappy dealers. How you choose to deal with your suppliers will often directly determine how well you can satisfy your customers. Suppliers, too, have needs and wants, hopes and fears.

What has been said about customers also applies to suppliers. In many businesses today, the higher you are in the value-adding process, the more dependent you really are on suppliers. This is as true for a dentist in solo practice as it is for a large manufacturer. As even very large corporations break into smaller units and others outsource many activities, the value of strong and effective supplier relationships will increase. The front line of those relationships are often people in purchasing, materials, or procurement functions. They are key links with your suppliers just as sales, service, and other contact people are links with customers.

Many companies spend a lot of time and money to train salespeople and customer-service specialists about how to effectively manage customer relationships. Very little is typically invested in teaching supplier-focused people how to usefully guide and enrich their vital contacts. As one consequence, most purchasing and materials experts know far less about their suppliers than they can and should. A useful place to begin is to examine the four characteristics of customers as they apply to suppliers.

What do your important suppliers need or want from you and your firm? What are their hopes and fears of doing business with you? How satisfied are supplier leaders, in an overall sense, with you as a customer? The same kinds of study methods described earlier can be very helpful. Surveys, face-to-face conversations, supplier employee focus groups, and cross-company, multifunction meetings are useful approaches. If the trading capability of your organization depends on outside suppliers, managing those linkages effectively is a vital leadership responsibility.

# Chapter 17

# Concluding Remarks

There is widespread and increasing confusion about what leadership of a business really is and how it fulfills its purpose. This confusion is reflected in statements of executives, government officials, and professors, no less than those of assembly-line workers and clerical employees.

Very few nongovernment organizations exist to provide jobs, pay high wages, or to be good corporate citizens. The large majority exist solely to trade, to transact with others. Providing jobs, funding socially approved projects, and, yes, even survival are *consequences* of successful trades. The business of business is trade, as true for services as for goods, and equally for professional practices and manufacturers. And it is just as true for a department or small firm as for a giant, worldwide company.

In every company of every size, there are already four architectural elements that can be converted by leaders into effective levers that will increase successful trade. Each is within the immediate reach of organization leaders. There are other elements, of course, but they are not easily defined, are hard to manipulate, and usually take a very long time to change. The levers of assets, systems, people, and organization are accessible and visible.

For these four elements to provide successful leverage over the longer term, they must be deliberately adjusted with high awareness of the firm's defining identity and the impact on employee self-confidence and respect. Four sources of self-esteem can be powerfully linked and energized in the service of organization purposes. Indeed, they must be if leader-driven change is to have either substantial or lasting positive outcomes.

- Achievement and accomplishment
- Recognition and being valued

- Power, control and influence
- Beliefs and values

Recent history shows the negative impact on company identity and performance on trade, when change is implemented that damages members' sense of self-worth and value. It can take years to overcome. Conversely, when an organization's key members experience a confident self-respect, they can and will overcome major performance barriers.

The ultimate purpose of change is to improve business performance through more successful trade, something that can only be achieved by satisfying customers. Customer needs and wants, hopes and fears, are all important. Each must be understood and resolved through persistent leader initiatives and the focused commitment of self-confident people.

This book has examined the features of organization architecture that can become the levers of change. It has examined the connections to member confidence and the resulting impact on the firm's identity and customer satisfaction, and on movement toward the destination of long-term, successful trade.

Even dramatic change can be successful when four conditions are met:

1. There is an unapologetic clarity and focus on trade as the company's sole purpose and reason to exist.
2. The levers are persistently engaged in inclusive, broadly communicated ways that sharpen and define the firm's identity.
3. Member commitment is a major concern of leaders; each confidence-building component is deliberately enhanced.
4. Key customers and suppliers are included; their needs and views are deliberately included throughout the process.

Leadership in business is more than technique or a series of tactical maneuvers. If it is only that, it may be very good management, but it is not leadership. In business, policy and strategy are closely related and depend ultimately on the assumptions, models, and ideologies, by which I mean values and beliefs, of leaders who create flexible paradigms about how things work, should work, or can be made to work. Many business leaders are accomplished strategists who rely on implicit models about human behavior, society, technology, and economics, among others. Their knowledge about such models derives inevitably from personal experiences, added to information from the short-term past organization successes and failures. But reliance on the recent past and on personal experience alone make for limited and not very flexible paradigms.

It is difficult for leaders to step outside of their own experiences and ideologies. For instance, increasing numbers of executives are technically trained, experienced, and educated. Many have developed a basic faith in technology, especially new technology, as the solution to problems of company strategy and policy. Other leaders display an ideology, a belief, about the "best way" to impel others to achieve. They are committed to their techniques as the answer to company strategy. Carried to an extreme, leader ideologies can be dangerous because, as with anyone's limited personal experiences, they can lead to inflexible models about how things work.

The most effective leaders I know are true to their values, their ideologies, but not slavishly so. For instance, such a leader may be personally committed to the ideology of technology and might direct many of the firm's assets to those purposes. But he or she will also deliberately engage the needs of the firm's people and invest significantly in better systems and processes throughout the enterprise.

Similarly, few executives have much personal experience with more than a very few companies, and personal experience is inevitably central to strategy development, as are leader beliefs and values. But overreliance on either alone can lead to narrow, inflexible models and flawed strategies.

A leader under heavy pressure will usually fall back on his or her beliefs and personal experiences in the search for solutions. Almost always, this drives a conviction about the potency of one particular architectural component as *the* lever of change. Whether the organization's design or its systems, the contribution of its people, or use of its assets is selected, pressured leaders will be predisposed to invest that component with their primary faith and confidence. I hope that the preceding exploration has been convincing. Creating real and lasting business improvement requires all four levers to be deliberately and, above all, persistently engaged.

# Index

Page numbers followed by the letter "f" indicate figures.

# Order Your Own Copy of
# This Important Book for Your Personal Library!

## 4 × 4 LEADERSHIP AND THE PURPOSE OF THE FIRM

_____ in hardbound at $49.95 (ISBN: 0-7890-0443-7)

_____ in softbound at $24.95 (ISBN: 0-7890-0444-5)

COST OF BOOKS_____

OUTSIDE USA/CANADA/
MEXICO: ADD 20%_____

POSTAGE & HANDLING_____
*(US: $3.00 for first book & $1.25
for each additional book)*
*Outside US: $4.75 for first book
& $1.75 for each additional book)*

SUBTOTAL_____

IN CANADA: ADD 7% GST_____

STATE TAX_____
*(NY, OH & MN residents, please
add appropriate local sales tax)*

**FINAL TOTAL**_____
*(If paying in Canadian funds,
convert using the current
exchange rate. UNESCO
coupons welcome.)*

☐ **BILL ME LATER:** ($5 service charge will be added)
(Bill-me option is good on US/Canada/Mexico orders only;
not good to jobbers, wholesalers, or subscription agencies.)

☐ Check here if billing address is different from
shipping address and attach purchase order and
billing address information.

Signature_____

☐ **PAYMENT ENCLOSED: $**_____

☐ **PLEASE CHARGE TO MY CREDIT CARD.**

☐ Visa   ☐ MasterCard   ☐ AmEx   ☐ Discover
☐ Diner's Club

Account # _____

Exp. Date _____

Signature _____

Prices in US dollars and subject to change without notice.

NAME _____

INSTITUTION _____

ADDRESS _____

CITY _____

STATE/ZIP _____

COUNTRY _____ COUNTY (NY residents only) _____

TEL _____ FAX _____

E-MAIL_____
May we use your e-mail address for confirmations and other types of information? ☐ Yes   ☐ No

*Order From Your Local Bookstore or Directly From*
**The Haworth Press, Inc.**
10 Alice Street, Binghamton, New York 13904-1580 • USA
TELEPHONE: 1-800-HAWORTH (1-800-429-6784) / Outside US/Canada: (607) 722-5857
FAX: 1-800-895-0582 / Outside US/Canada: (607) 772-6362
E-mail: getinfo@haworth.com
PLEASE PHOTOCOPY THIS FORM FOR YOUR PERSONAL USE.

BOF96

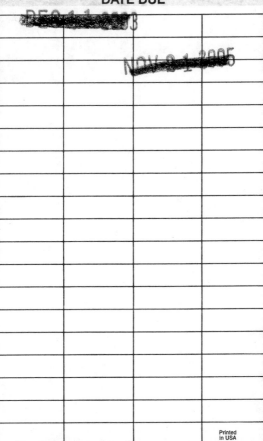

DATE DUE

DEC 1 1 2003

NOV 2 1 2005